Men-at-Arms • 288

American Indians of the Southeast

Michael Johnson • Illustrated by Richard Hook

Series editor Martin Windrow

First published in Great Britain in 1995 by Osprey Publishing,
Midland House, West Way, Botley, Oxford OX2 0PH, UK
443 Park Avenue South, New York, NY 10016, USA
Email: info@ospreypublishing.com

CIP Data for this publication is available from
the British Library

ISBN 978 1 85532 566 1

08 09 10 11 12 17 16 15 14 13 12 11 10 9 8

Series Editor: MARTIN WINDROW
Filmset in Great Britain by KDI
Printed in China through World Print Ltd.

FOR A CATALOGUE OF ALL BOOKS PUBLISHED BY
OSPREY MILITARY AND AVIATION PLEASE CONTACT:

NORTH AMERICA
Osprey Direct, C/o Random House Distribution Centre,
400 Hahn Road, Westminster, MD 21157
Email: info@ospreydirect.com

ALL OTHER REGIONS
Osprey Direct, The Book Service Ltd, Distribution
Centre, Colchester Road, Frating Green, Colchester,
Essex, CO7 7DW
E-mail: customerservice@ospreypublishing.com

www.ospreypublishing.com

Author's dedication

The author dedicates this book to William (Will) Reid
of Birmingham, England.

Acknowledgements

The author would like to thank Timothy O'Sullivan
and Denise Payne for their help in the preparation of
the text and Dr William C. Sturtevant of the
Smithsonian Institution, Washington DC, who made a
number of suggestions on the selection of appropriate
tribal dress for the plates.

Artist's note

Readers may care to note that the original paintings
from which the colour plates in this book were prepared are available for private sale. All reproduction
copyright whatsoever is retained by the publisher. All
enquiries should be addressed to:

Scorpio Gallery
PO Box 475
Hailsham
E. Sussex BN27 2SL

The publishers regret that they can enter into no
correspondence upon this matter.

AMERICAN INDIANS OF THE SOUTHEAST

INTRODUCTION

The native peoples of the southeastern United States have often been neglected or ignored in popular imagery of the North American Indian, yet they were prominent in the early history of the continent, being caught in the web of colonial intrigue between Great Britain, France and Spain. Tragically, the coastal tribes diminished rapidly through the introduction of European diseases contracted from the early expeditions of white explorers and Spanish missions. The interior trans-Appalachian south was the home of larger tribes, who had become involved in the mercantile activities of white traders, and the exchange of deer hides for European technology, including guns, metal objects and domestic animals, saw the development of several important culturally hybrid communities.

The southeastern people were the descendants of ancient prehistoric Indian cultures, and were probably on the decline when first known to Europeans. Despite being poorly reported in popular histories, they have been well described by several early European traders and by a number of well-known American ethnologists, including James Mooney and John R. Swanton, who collected and recorded details of surviving native culture in the late 19th and early 20th centuries. The white man's expanding plantation society and the tragic removal of the Indian population to Indian Territory saw the end of this farming, hunting and trading culture.

Photography developed too late to catch outstanding images of native culture, so our plates are partly dependent upon the work of early artists, descriptions by white explorers and traders, and the remains of material culture in our museums.

Prehistoric native people of eastern North America

At least 15,000 years ago small bands of Stone Age hunters ventured into the wilderness we now know as North America, then covered by thousands of square miles of ice hundreds of feet thick as far south as the present Great Lakes. To the south, beyond the ice-line in the eastern United States, pine, hemlock, oak, chestnut and hickory flourished in a cooler and damper climate than today. There lived large game animals – mammoths, mastodons, horses, camels and Ice Age bison – all of which became extinct.

It seems that these Ice Age hunters had spread from the Old World – from Asia to Alaska, Canada, and then further south. These were the Stone Age Paleo-Indians. They may have been a pre-Mongoloid race, and they have left us distinctive cutting tools with grooves and flutes that have been classified as *Folsom* and *Clovis* from modern place names in New Mexico where paleolithic sites have been found. The Clovis-type spear-points are the type most commonly found by archaeologists in the eastern United States, but organic materials suitable for radio-carbon dating are often lacking in Ice Age sites, so information about these hunters is meagre, and the date or occupation of sites and the age of man in the New World is a matter of some debate. Some scientists put the date of the appearance of man in North America beyond 20,000 years ago.

The Paleo-Indian period seems to have come to an end about 6,000 years ago. By this time the glaciers had melted away, leaving the great rivers and lakes we know today. The big game animals too, gradually disappeared. In the eastern half of the continent the forests grew thick, and the changing environment of the early post-glacial period saw the arrival of a Mesolithic (Middle Stone Age) people characterised by the use of plant foods, nuts, fruit and shellfish. They had chipped weapons and hunting implements of flint or similar stone, which were made with greater precision; they used spear throwers, fish hooks and bone awls, had woven fabrics, shell ornaments and beads, pounded copper in flat sheets, ground seeds, and used dogs for work and for rituals. This period is known as the Archaic period.

Archaic sites of as late as around 1000 BC are

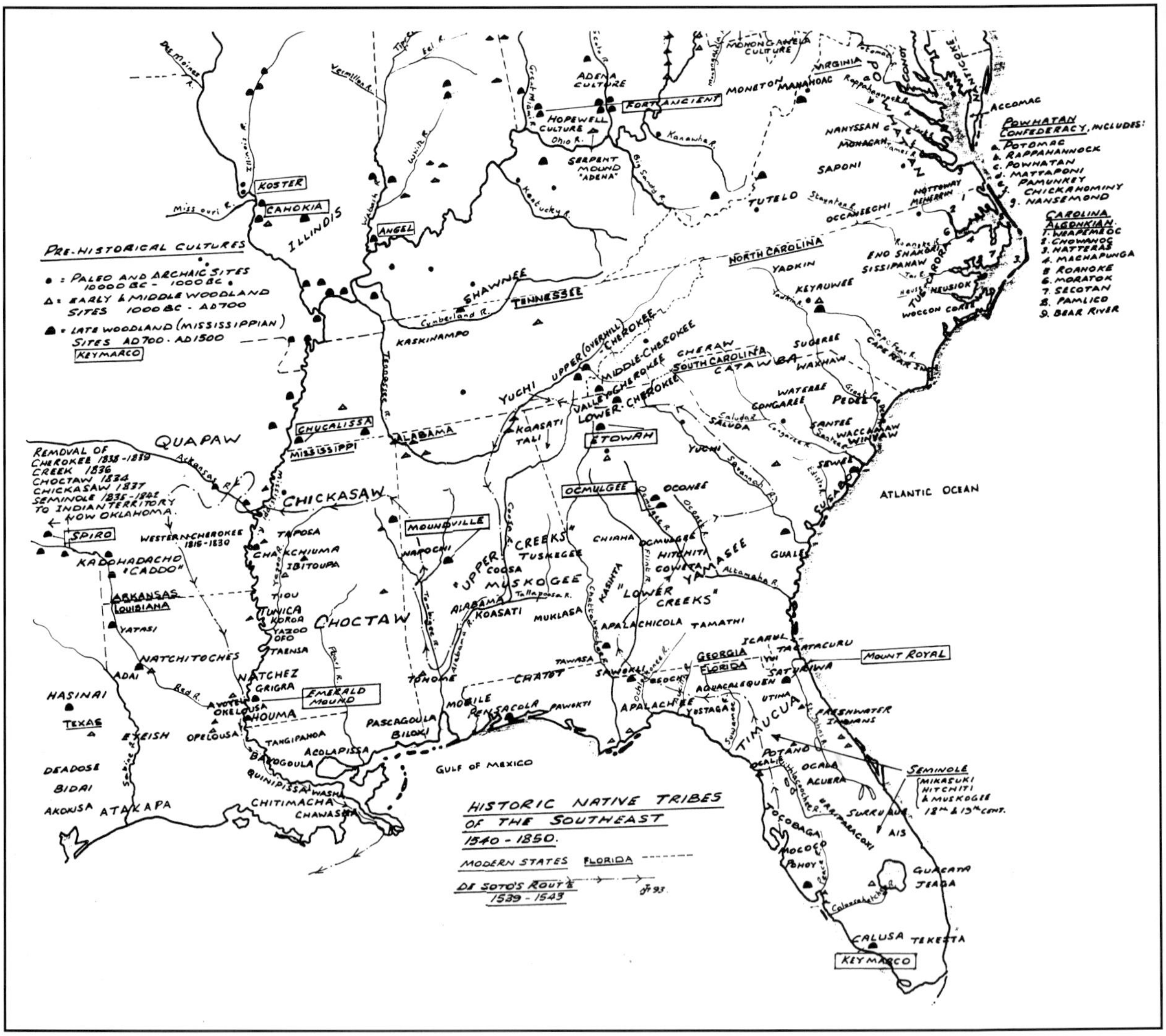

Historic native tribes of the southeast 1540–1850.

found throughout the east of the country. The Archaic period overlapped several periods of cultural development called Late Archaic, Transitional and Early Woodland. The Early Woodland people, on the evidence of skeletal remains, looked similar to the Archaic people and were Mongoloid in appearance; as yet the only clear criterion for distinguishing Late Archaic cultures from Early Woodland is the presence of ceramics in the later archaeological sites. During the Early Woodland period mortuary ceremonialism seems to have developed, with cremation burial mounds of earth in (at first) small conical and (later) huge effigy forms. Various local cultures have been defined (known as a Complex, Phase or Aspect), each with its own ceramics of clay or steatite, Red Ochre, Old Copper and Adena from around 1000 BC are the better known phases of these cultures.

The Adenas builders of the famous Serpent Mound of Ohio were a tall people with large round skulls, different from the Paleo and the longheaded early-Archaic Indian. This has led some archaeologists to believe they may have been immigrants from Mexico, and may have brought with them the beginnings of agriculture. There is little doubt that maize, beans and squash came to the American midwest, along with the art of their cultivation and associated myths, from the south, via the Gilmore Corridor in Texas and other routes. Pottery designs are also similar to those on Mexican stone carvings.

These late Archaic periods climaxed with the Hopewell culture of around 300 BC. This was the so-called Middle Woodland period, and saw the development of maize (Indian corn) agriculture, which had spread into the Ohio Valley indirectly from Middle America. The Hopewell people built the most impressive burial mounds of the New World: earth embankments formed enclosures in which burial mounds were arranged. The dominant theme in their culture was the preparation for death, and rich treasures were consigned to tombs over which great earthen mounds were built as everlasting monuments. Ornaments, pipes, tools, weapons, polished stone, mica and cord impressed, corn and mortuary vessels have been recovered from Hopewell sites. From its centre in Ohio Hopewell cultural influence spread as far as Florida – and as far west as Oklahoma. This has been viewed as a developmental peak, and later Woodland cultures appear to have been in decline. Hopewell culture disappeared about AD 700.

The Late Woodland period is called 'Mississippian', from the valley where its development occurred. Probably inspired by new ideas from Mexico, the Mississippian people constructed large flat-topped earth pyramids, which served as platforms for temples, and buildings with thatched roofs. The Temple Mound culture, with its complex farming, ceremonial arts and crafts and the religious activities (called the Southern Death Cult or Buzzard Cult) spread throughout the east and south. The basic foods were corn, beans, squash and a variety of nuts, seeds and berries, supplemented by elk, bear, raccoon, molluscs and turkey. The Mississippian culture appeared about AD 700 and lasted, although in decline, until the arrival of the earliest European explorers. The Mississippians' best known sites are Cahokia, Aztalan, Fort Ancient (also previously a Hopewell site), in the south, Etowah and Ocmulgee, and in the west, Spiro, Oklahoma. Both the Hopewell Burial Mound peoples and the later Mississippian Temple Mound peoples had intense trading links and routes throughout eastern North America, which facilitated the spread of the trappings of their cultures: elaborate ornaments, pipes, tools, weapons and vessels.

Mississippian towns were usually established on an island or near a river. A plaza was laid out, with several houses and temples enclosed by a palisade.

Dwellings were constructed of long saplings set upright in trenches, and the roof framework was woven like a huge basket. The exterior surfaces of the walls were lathed with cane and plastered with clay. Temples seem to have been built over demolished or outworn council chambers: the flat-topped pyramids becoming the foundation for the temples. Elsewhere, entire hilltops were levelled off and terraced to create plazas, with temple mounds built on top. These traditions and building activities reflect Central American influences, although the architectural results were more primitive. In some areas temple-mound building became associated with the Death Cult or Buzzard Cult, so called because those who practised it were preoccupied with death. A great proliferation of skilfully made grave goods accompanied the spread of the cult – copper plaques, ear spools, axes, pottery and shell – all engraved with intricate symbolic designs. Human sacrifice was also practised, another trait that was probably of Meso-American origin.

With dramatic suddenness mound building ceased and the whole culture associated with it waned. Perhaps the shock of European invasion spread panic and sealed the fate of a culture already in decline. The historic Indian peoples who succeeded the Mississippians, when questioned about their mound-building ancestors, seemed to know little of their predecessors, although cultural traits clearly did survive. The annual rekindling of the sacred fire, an earthly symbol of the Sun, colour symbolism and the *Puskita* or *Busk* (a kind of New Year or world renewal celebration which took place when the corn ripened) were all descended from the Temple Mound culture.

The Natchez people were probably the only tribe to have survived to the 17th century with a form of Mississippian culture largely intact and to have been seen by Europeans. They were ruled by a living deity, the Great Sun, who lived in a structure on top of a pyramid earth mound in the tribe's primary village. His residence was burned at his death, and the mound was then made bigger and a new residence for his successor built directly on top of it. The temple mound was built adjacent to the Great Sun's house. The temple itself, a structure of cypress logs, was divided into two rooms; one housed the eternal fire, the other the remains of the Great Sun's predecessor in a cane coffin. The Great Sun's mother was White Woman, the direct descendant of the original Great Sun. She lived luxuriously, was carried on a litter, wore magnificent feather cloaks and ate the finest foods. Her first-born son became the future Great Sun, and her first daughter the next White Woman. At her death her husband – a commoner – and a number of other men and women were executed to accompany her to the spirit world.

Our knowledge of prehistoric ceremonial dress comes from scenes engraved on shell gorgets that were worn or hung around the neck. They were recovered from archaeological sites such as Spiro (Oklahoma) and Etowah (Georgia) and display engraved designs depicting dancers and conventionalised rattlesnake and bird designs. Spiro figures are often stiffer than those of Etowah; faces show the so-called 'weeping eye' design seen on masks. Copper, also used as a medium for ceremonial art, seems to have been traded in from the north, perhaps via the Caddoan peoples, and was made into ceremonial plaques of thin sheets. Designs depicting eagle and buzzard costumed dancers were made by cutting and indenting. Earlier, the Hopewell peoples of the Ohio country had hammered copper into large ornaments in the shape of snake heads, birds and double-headed birds. The southeastern people also produced impressive stone carvings of human figures, tubular pipes in the forms of birds and animals, and great stone effigy pipes. A small group of wooden sculptures recovered from the Marco Island site in Florida are also remarkable, possibly the work of the Calusa people, adding to the diverse ceremonial art of the region.

Tribes of the southeast

European contact with the tribes began with the Spanish explorers, notably the expedition of Hernando de Soto during 1539–43. He and his 700 troops proved to be the angel of death for the native peoples: they brought disease, disrupted Indian life, enslaved numbers of people and were a drain on food resources. The Spanish moved from Tampa Bay, Florida, northwards, advancing up the Savannah River in present-day Georgia, where he made prisoner the 'queen' of a town called Cofitachiqui. De Soto then seems to have passed through territory of the Sara (*Cheraw*) tribe, and crossed the Blue Ridge into Cherokee territory in his search for gold. After four years of wandering – to the Great Plains and back to the Mississippi River – De Soto died, and his body was consigned to that great river. Only 300 of his original army arrived in Mexico in 1543.

The effects of Spanish activity and French Huguenot colonies (South Carolina in 1561 and Florida in 1562, subsequently taken over by the Spanish) and their establishment of missions such as St. Augustine, Florida, and Juan Pardo's expedition of 1567 – which probably reached the limits of Cherokee country – began a decline of the native population, particularly among the tribes in close contact with the new arrivals. A total population of perhaps half a million had been reduced to half that number by the 17th century.

Ethnologists and linguists have divided the tribes that survived the initial European impact into 13 sub-groups, largely based on language affiliation. Reference to the map for the smaller tribes within each section should be made, as they are too numerous to be listed individually.

1. Algonkians

The Algonkian tribes of Virginia and North Carolina are related to the tribes to the north. The *Powhatans* were a confederacy in the Tidewater area of present-day Virginia, along the James, York and Rappahannock rivers. They were so named from their great chieftain, Powhatan, at the time of the English settlement at Jamestown in 1607. The

Tobacco pouch, Creek, Georgia 18th century, made from an alligator's foot. (Courtesy Saffron Walden Museum, UK)

Powhatans were engaged in two tragic wars with colonists – in 1622 and 1644 – which largely destroyed them. A few descendants still exist today. A second group, of several tribes of Algonkians, who are famous for their connection with the early English colony on Roanoke Island, North Carolina, in 1585–87, were recorded in the paintings of John White. The largest groups were the *Weapemeoc* and *Chawanoke*, now extinct. For a number of years, a band of the Algonkian Shawnee lived on the Savannah River.

2. Iroquoians

There were two groups of these people, relatives of the Iroquois who had separated from their northern kinsmen perhaps 700 years ago. There were small tribes in Virginia, the *Nottaway* and the *Meherrin*, and a larger body, the *Tuscarora*, on the Roanoke, Neuse, Tar and Pamlico rivers of North Carolina. The *Tuscarora* fought two wars against the English colonists of North Carolina between 1711 and 1713. Chief Hencock rebelled against the colonists for the enslavement of Indians and encroachment on their lands and captured the explorer, John Lawson and Baron de Graffenried. However, Barnwell's colonist army, aided by Yamasee and other tribes, defeated the *Tuscarora* so badly that many of their members left the area, journeyed north and joined the Iroquois league.

Among the cultural features of this region were wigwams, longhouses, dependence on fish, matrilineal descent, some female chiefs, burial in the ground or in ossuaries, tattooing, the use of shell ornamentation and the custom among men of shaving their hair from one side of the head and allowing full growth on the other.

3. Siouans

The largest of the Siouan-speaking peoples of the east (distantly related to the Siouan-speaking Plains Indians) were the *Catawba* (and a number of minor tribes below them in South Carolina who became incorporated into the *Catawba* during the 18th century), the *Pedee* (and others) who occupied rivers where the two Carolinas now meet, and the warlike *Cheraw* in northern South Carolina. To the north were the *Eno* branch on the upper courses of the Black, Cape Fear, Neuse and Haw rivers in North

Captain John Smith trading with the Powhatan Indians on the James River, Virginia, in 1607. Jamestown was the first permanent English colony in the New World.

Diorama. (National History Museum, Smithsonian Institution, Washington DC, USA, photograph M.G. Johnson)

Kish-kal-wa, a Shawnee chief c. 1826. The Shawnee, an Algonkian people, were only marginal to the southeast: a portion of them had lived in the Savannah River country during the 18th century, affiliated

with the Creeks. Their customs and dress reflected this connection. From a lithograph published by McKenney and Hall (1836–1944) derived from a painting by Charles Bird King.

Carolina and the *Tutelo-Saponi* of Virginia's Piedmont region. Most of these separate groups disappeared in the 18th century, except for the *Catawba* and a body of mixed racial groups. Old traders reported the prominence of female chiefs, puberty rites, wooden images and slaves. In the 17th century two Siouan groups lived in the far south – the *Biloxi*, around the bay which bears their name, and the *Ofo*, near the Mississippi River.

4. Yamasee

One of the many Muskogian-speaking tribes of the southeast, the Yamasee lived from the Savannah River country to Florida, and were no doubt connected to the coastal *Cusabo* and others. The Spanish missionised the coastal groups, who then suffered English and Indian attacks from the north as a consequence. The Yamasee themselves were engaged in a disastrous war with the English in 1715, and largely disappeared from history, save for a few who joined the Seminole in Florida.

5. Florida tribes

The *Timucua* of northern Florida and the *Calusa* of southern Florida may have spoken languages unrelated to the Muskogian tongues so dominant further north. *Timucua* life was recorded by an artist who accompanied French settlers to Florida in the 16th century. They were an agricultural people (the *Calusa* were hunters and fishermen). *Timucua* women used Spanish moss as clothing, and men sometimes kept their hair long and tied up on top. Rectangular lodges were covered with palmetto thatching, and alligators were used as food. They had totemic clans and probably a caste system. The *Timucua* were drawn into the mission system and diminished through diseases and raids by Indians from the north under British control. The last of the *Calusa* may have crossed to Cuba or joined the Seminoles. In northwest Florida were the *Apalachee*, a large and powerful Muskogian people, who were gathered into mission towns which were largely destroyed by Creek or *Yuchi* under British influence.

6. Creek Confederacy

A large grouping of Muskogian tribes, sometimes known collectively as Muskogee or Muskogi, who were divided into two sections, the Lower Creeks on the Chattahoochee, Flint and Ocmulgee rivers in Georgia (*Kasihta* and *Coweta*) and the Upper Creeks on the Alabama, Coosa and Tallapoosa rivers of Alabama. As the nation became involved in colonial struggles, other tribes gradually affiliated with them. The *Hitchiti, Okmulgee, Mikasuki* and others joined the Lower Creeks, whilst the *Alabama, Koasati* and *Tuskegee* became Upper Creeks. The *Yuchi* tribe, who, though linguistically unrelated, also joined the Creeks at various times, were originally from the Savannah River country. The Seminole, who were descended from Lower and Upper Creeks, immigrated to Florida in the 18th and 19th century. The Creeks generally were friendly with the British Carolinas.

7. Choctaw and Chickasaw

Two closely related Muskogian tribes of Mississippi who were usually in a state of inter-tribal warfare were the Choctaw and the Chickasaw. The latter, of northern Mississippi and Tennessee, were noted for their independent and warlike character, and refused all French advances, preferring an association with British traders. The Choctaw occupied present day central Mississippi and Alabama west of the Tombigbee River. They were matrilineal, and were divided into towns and districts, each ruled by chiefs. The Choctaw were also noted for their long hair, artificial head deformation, bark covered lodges, scaffold burial and the use of the calumet ceremony (the 'peace pipe') to cement friendship and treaties, perhaps adopted from tribes in the northern Mississippi Valley. A large number of minor tribes can, for convenience, be added to the Choctaw group. There were groups on the Yazoo River (*Chakchiuma*), on the lower Mississippi River, in Louisiana (*Bayogoula, Houma*) and in north-eastern Florida (*Pensacola, Mobile*), and an ancient tribe, the *Napochi*, who once lived on Black Warrior River. Of these smaller groups only the *Houma*, mixed with French Creoles, have survived in the Mississippi Delta.

8. Natchez

Three tribes formed this divergent Muskogian group about St. Catharine's Creek, Mississippi, and were noted for a peculiar caste organisation where high caste members were compelled to marry commoners and chiefs were considered to be descendants of a solar culture hero. They were defeated by the French in 1729, and many were sold into slavery or joined other tribes and consequently became almost extinct.

9. Tunica

A group of tribes who occupied the valley of the Mississippi River in Louisiana and Mississippi, the Tunica were noted for their skill in dressing skins and producing fine pottery. The group is perhaps distantly related to the Muskogians. A few descendants remain in Louisiana.

10. Chitimacha

A group of three tribes who lived about the delta of the Mississippi and Grande Lake, Louisiana, who had cultural similarities with the Natchez and perhaps were related to the Tunica and Muskogians. They often killed enemies by poisoning water, and had a great dependence on fish and alligators for food. They excelled in basketry. A few descendants survive in Louisiana.

11. Atakapa

A group of small tribes of the gulf coast of Texas, sometimes included in the southeastern cultural area. Linguistically they may be distantly related to the *Chitimacha* and *Tunica*, but have been long extinct as a tribal group, though a few Creole descendants may remain.

12. Caddo

The south-eastern part of the Caddoan family, whose range beyond this region included parts of the Missouri Valley, lived in northern Louisiana and adjacent Texas and Oklahoma and were drawn into the frontier economy brought in by French traders in the 17th and 18th centuries. They lived in thatched grass houses, were potters, and traded bows for salt. Unlike many tribes tattooing was not common among them. They formed small confederacies which gradually combined into one people – Caddo – who finally settled in Indian Territory, where a few hundred of their number remain. To the north of the Caddo were the *Quapaw*, a Siouan people, whose culture reflected their geographical position between the southeastern and Plains areas.

A Creek man painted by Lukas Vischer in 1824, probably in Alabama, shows the typical hybrid dress of the period prior to their removal to Indian territory. He is shown wearing a cloth tunic, turban, probably finger-woven woollen belt and knee garters. (Photograph courtesy of Professor Christian F. Feest)

13. Cherokee

The largest tribe of the southeast were the Cherokee. Their language was a very divergent Iroquoian tongue, indicating a long separation from their northern kinsmen. They formed a nation of over 60 towns in the areas around the head-waters of the Tennessee, Savannah and Coosa rivers. Archaeological evidence suggests they were long-time inhabitants of the area, and we may conclude that their ancestors were mound builders. The Cherokee were expert potters and basket makers. Ancient ceremonial dress of leaders and priests included feather cloaks and elaborate head-dresses of swan, crane and other feathers. During the 18th century their culture became increasingly Europeanised, and they became expert metalworkers and gunsmiths. In Oklahoma they ultimately became perhaps the most acculturated American Indian people.

Tribes that remain

Only the Cherokee, Creek, Choctaw, Chickasaw and Seminole have survived in numbers to the present day, principally in Oklahoma, the 'Indian Territory' to which their ancestors were moved in the first half of the 19th century. They formed the so-called 'Five Civilized Tribes' and had some degree of independence, until the Civil War and ultimately statehood engulfed them. Under leaders of mixed European and Indian descent, they became Americanised dur-

Steechacomeco, also called 'Ben Perryman', a distinguished Creek leader painted by George Catlin near Fort Gibson

Indian Territory c. 1834–38. He wears a triangular flap pouch that was very popular with Creek men at the time.

ing the 19th century, with few native institutions remaining except among conservative Creeks. A number escaped removal to Oklahoma: some Choctaw remained in Mississippi; a few Creeks in Alabama; Eastern Cherokees in North Carolina; and Seminoles in Florida, until recently, the most conservative and isolated of all. The smaller tribes mostly disappeared and merged into the larger Oklahoma groups, but a few *Yuchi* (Oklahoma), *Koasati* (Louisiana), *Alabama* (Texas) and *Houma, Tunica* and *Chitimacha* (Louisiana) survive, all much mixed with other races. In the Carolinas and Virginia are considerable numbers of people reflecting the hybrid nature of frontier life of the past. The Lumbee (North Carolina), Summerville (South Carolina) and Powhantan (Virginia) are people descended from a mixed tribal and racial background but without tribal traditions, which were probably exchanged for those of frontier people, both white and black, in the 18th century. These groups have insisted upon social separation from blacks, and

form a sizeable, if somewhat submerged, racial group. Of those Federally recognised as Indian, about 150,000 remain, a sizeable increase in recent times, but well below their original numbers.

Indian culture and traditions of the southeast

The aboriginal culture of the interior tribes of the southeast was one of the most advanced of any native American society outside Mexico. Subsistence was based partially on agriculture, specifically corn (maize), beans and squashes, but the natives also collected sunflower seeds and berries and were hunters and fishermen. Women usually organised the agriculture such as the planting and cultivation of crops. They also made clothing, pottery and baskets, dressed skins, collected firewood and cooked. Men made bows and war clubs, hunted, built houses, and attended to war and trading expeditions through a network of Indian trails throughout the region.

The Indians were far more travelled than is generally supposed; highly probable accounts relate visits to friendly tribes 1,000 to 2,000 miles away and equally long journeys for war or adventure. Great Indian trails covered the whole area, following routes of least natural resistance, sometimes along old game trails and salt licks, and often paralleling water routes. Material objects such as pipes, mica, dentalium shells and copper, encouraged a wide network of trade in prehistoric and early historic times. The Great Indian Warpath (see map) ran from Creek country in Alabama through the Cherokee country of East Tennessee, with one branch proceeding into Virginia, Pennsylvania and beyond. The other branch led via the Holston, New and Kanawha rivers to the Ohio country. Many Iroquois war parties passed along it to strike as far south as northern Alabama.

Although dug-out canoes were widely used, most travel was on foot or, later, by horse. Water travel was more common along the coasts of the Gulf of Mexico, Florida and the Atlantic Ocean, particularly in areas of lagoons. On some interior rivers, canoes of elm or cypress bark occasionally replaced heavier dug-outs, particularly when travelling upstream.

Most of the doctors, prophets and warchiefs were men, although occasionally women also rose to

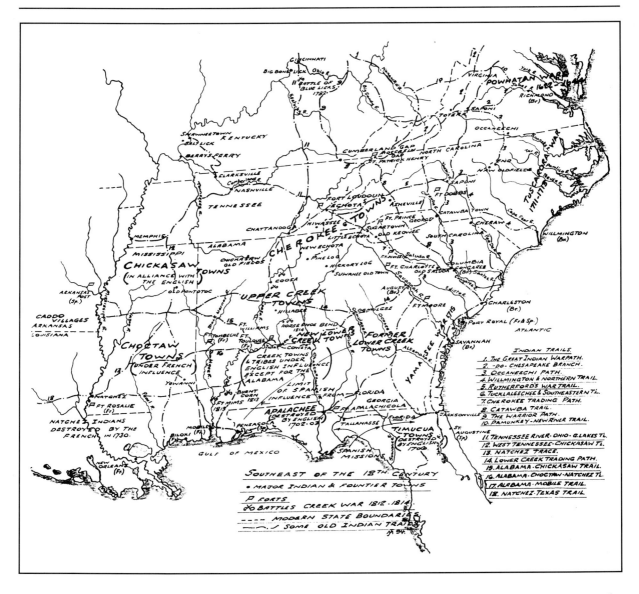

Southeast of the 18th century.

the position of chieftainess. Among the *Tunica* tribes men also assumed the duties connected with the cultivation of the cornfields. Religion was a complex of reverence for the Sun, Fire and Great Serpent cults, and no doubt had descended from the Mississippian culture. Religious belief among some tribes seems to have culminated in the concept of a high god or supreme deity connected with the Sun, and a multitude of lesser spirits. There also seem to have been separate classes of priests, prophets and doctors.

Although the details differ from tribe to tribe, some southeastern peoples (Cherokee) believed the universe was divided into three separate parts: the Upper World of perfect order, This World, where humankind lived together with the animals and plants, and the Lower World of disorder, evil and pollution, but also of fertility and invention. In the beginning, only the Upper and Lower Worlds existed; This World developed from the constant struggle between the Upper and Lower worlds and man, animals and plants hovered between them. Four-footed animals and birds sometimes interchanged between This World and the Upper World. Snakes, lizards and fish were all part of the Lower World, as was the great *Uktena*, the Cherokee mythological monster snake which had a bright crystal or diamond on its head. Indians had a strong belief in

Shawnee Green Corn Dance, Whiteoak, Oklahoma, 1969. The Shawnee were marginal to the southeastern area and a part of the tribe (Saluda) had lived in the Savannah River country for some generations in the 18th century. They ultimately found a home in Oklahoma. Their old culture, traditions and art reflected their juxtaposition between the northeastern and southeastern woodlands. (Photograph James H. Howard)

conjurors, healers and medicine men using divining crystals (thought to have been from the scales of the *Uktena*), but only one crystal talisman, wrapped in a deerskin and hidden in a cave, had been reported among the North Carolina Cherokee by 1900.

The Cherokee had a theory that disease was based on the natural world's revenge for the contempt and carelessness of humans towards animals. Plants, herbs and trees, friendly to man, were enlisted to check disease. Emetic drinks, herbal drugs and stimulants were widely used for ceremonial purification, and pain relief and personal herbal medicines were often carried or smoked. The so-called 'Black Drink', also called 'Carolina Tea' by whites, was a caffeine-laden emetic and purgative used for purification at the Green Corn Festival and is still used by the Florida Seminole. The latter, until recently, also had active medicine men – keepers of a deerskin medicine bundle opened each year at the festival – and occasionally practised purifying by scarification as protection for the year to come; scratching was usually on the arms. Fear of ghosts, and belief in 'spirit helpers', usually animals, and dreams were endemic.

The Sun was the greatest deity represented on earth, through fire. Worship of the Sun God, along with the social class systems, suggests a pervasive influence of Mississippian culture and ultimately of Meso-America. Most tribes built and maintained a sacred fire.

The southeastern peoples viewed themselves as an integral part of the natural world that was filled with infinite varieties of plants, animals, insects and stones, each with numerous myths surrounding them and possessing spirit force; some animals even took on the characteristics of humans and were considered as 'tribes'.

Cherokee myths suggest that originally the people emerged from the waters of the underworld, with equal status with animals – a concept widely held by Native Americans. The Cherokee had six great festivals each year, held in special council houses in each major town. They celebrated the Planting of Corn in the spring, the First Green Crop in August, the Ripe Green Corn Feast in September, the October feasts of New Moon and Reconciliation and the Bounding Bush Feast in December.

The Creek's most important ceremonial was also a Green Corn Ceremony or *Puskita*, a 'fast' or *Busk*, as it was termed by white traders. It was an annual festival which helped unify town, tribe and nation. Ideas of peace, law, friendship and atonement of sin accompanied the ritual, which took place in a town square and lasted between four and eight days. It was usually held in the 'white' or 'peace' towns as opposed to the 'red' towns, where war ceremonies were performed. *Busks* were under the direction of a *Mico* (chief) and his assistants. The ritual part of the Green Corn Ceremony included the world renewal rite – the kindling of a new fire between four logs set upon the ground in the form of a cross, with reference to the four cardinal points. Men who performed some

Modern Cherokees demonstrating the use of the blowgun at a competition at the old Cherokee capital of New Echota, Georgia c. 1985. (Photograph by Guy Wood)

of the rituals drank emetic brews that produced vomiting as a form of ceremonial purification; alternatively purification could be obtained by deep scratching of the skin.

Micos or priests invoked the Master of Breath deity by offering an ear of corn over the sacred fire at dawn while facing the rising sun, thus consecrating the new harvest, or by ritual use of ashes, water, salt, pine boughs or, long ago, by copper plates embossed with mythical designs that were laid in the sand altars reflecting the sun and representing the image of the Master of Breath. The new fire meant new life, moral and physical. Everything used during the *Busk* had to be new, including clothes, to renew the world, its seasons and the agricultural calendar. Versions of this ceremonial, one of the most important of Native American rituals, were practised from the Florida Seminoles to the New York Iroquois, and is still performed by Seminoles and Creeks. The ceremonials resembled those of ancient Mexico, and underlined fundamental elements of southeastern Indian culture.

Dances for men and women were accompanied by turtle shell rattles worn on the legs, sometimes gourd rattles, and drums. Tribal dances were almost always performed around the central fire at the opening of medicine bundles for tribal well-being.

Slaves were not widely used in the southeast except during the 18th and 19th centuries when the Indians were drawn into the economic culture brought by whites. Choctaw, Creek and Seminoles held black slaves (the Seminoles welcomed black runaways as military auxiliaries against Americans). Captives were sometimes killed but sometimes adopted.

Material culture, dress and ornamentation

Houses varied across the southeast. The Cherokee lived in houses built of poles set vertically in the ground then interwoven with twigs covered with a mixture of clay and grass. Creek dwellings were often four houses in a square, sometimes a mixture of dwelling houses and food storage structures. These grouped houses surrounded the area of the ceremonial council house, public square and game yard where the rituals and *Chunkey* games were held. The modern Creek Indian square grounds in Oklahoma are ceremonial sites, and the remnant of such village arrangements.

The domestic dwellings were often the property of the women of the family, and married girls would continue to occupy ancestral dwellings, or others erected for them, in the family neighbourhood. In the north, among the *Powhatan*, wigwams resembling those of the North Woodlands were used, and summer houses of the Carolina tribes were little more than open pavilions. In the Gulf area thatched houses of palmetto were used – the Seminole of the Florida peninsula continued, and developed, raised *Chickees* derived from earlier dwellings of the *Timucua* and *Calusa*. In the west, Caddo dwellings were thatched with grass, as were the roofs of

Chickasaw winter houses. *Quapaw* and *Yazoo* houses were sometimes covered with cypress bark or palmetto. During the 18th century log structures were adopted from white frontiersmen, and in the 19th century, rich Cherokee and Creek mixed-bloods lived in fine Southern-style mansions.

Canoes were used throughout the region, and were constructed of logs hollowed out with fire. The Seminole of Florida used cypress logs for their canoes, which could be projected through the shallow waters of the swamps with poles, and occasionally they built rafts of cane. Horses were adopted for travel, and whites introduced domesticated animals during the 18th century.

The Cherokee and *Catawba* are famous for their split-cane basketry and pottery, as well as for elaborately carved stone pipes. Before the Gulf and other southeastern tribes had guns, they used bows and arrows for hunting. Favourite woods for bows were black locust, sassafras and cedar. Quivers were of either skin or cane.

Material culture and native attire often disappeared within a few generations of European contact, so it is difficult to determine true aboriginal regional or tribal differences in dress or ornamentation, and relatively little has survived in museum collections. Male attire often consisted only of a breechclout of deerskin or later of cloth passed between the legs and over a belt. The belt was sometimes of snakeskin. Men covered their upper bodies with garments made from skins of the bear, deer, panther and, sometimes, bison. The latter, not usually associated with the technology of the southeastern tribes, was at one time numerous in the western region of the area. In the early 18th century Natchez men were described as dressed in deerskins which resembled the white man's jackets and descended halfway down the thighs. The making of buckskin men's shirts remained among the Tunica of Louisiana until recent times, and southeastern tanning has a reputation for fine quality. The trader Adair also reported deerskin male garments and European-style ruffled shirts of linen in the 18th century. Apparently, cloaks of feathers and skins were also widely used by both sexes. Women's cloaks were sometimes spun from the inner bark of the mulberry tree, grasses or Spanish moss. Leading men wore headbands of feather, skins or metals;

Basket of split cane, from the Carolinas, probably Cherokee 18th century. (Courtesy of the Museum of Mankind, British Museum)

later, headbands or handkerchiefs purchased from white traders were used – so-called turbans. Like most native Americans, southeastern Indians extracted facial hair, but some tribes, like the *Keyauwee* men of the upper Yadkin River, wore moustaches or whiskers. The Choctaw often wore their hair long, but Chickasaw and Creek men shaved the head, leaving a roach or crest reddened with puccoon root; others wore braids. Some articles of clothing were decorated with native beads of wampum, perhaps traded from the north, or Roanoke wampum, a shell from the Carolinas and Virginia. Ears were slit and decorated with conch shells or silver pendants. Nose-rings and crescent-shaped breast ornaments were also worn. In cold weather, and to protect limbs from the underbrush, buckskin leggings and moccasins were used. Cherokee, Creek and Seminole moccasins are of the type widely known in eastern North America, each cut from a single piece of buckskin and with a centre instep and heel. The seams were laced together, with heavy crimping at the front. The moccasin extended up the leg and was bound with a thong to hold it in position.

Reports and sketches made of Florida Indians in the 16th century show both sexes nearly naked, often tattooed, women with long hair and wearing fringed skirts, and men wearing earrings, carrying large fans and wearing cloaks. Carolina *Algonkan* women, also sketched in 1585–87, wore skirts of deerskin and

These are typical eastern one-piece buckskin moccasins (probably Creek or Cherokee, c. 1830) with beadwork in the style of the southeastern tribes. (John W. Painter Collection, Ohio, USA)

A rare group of objects from the southeastern Indians (probably Cherokee and Choctaw) were donated to the present Marischal Museum, University of Aberdeen, Scotland, before 1840, and probably date c. 1790. The old inventory notes materials 'furnished by the traders' but the work of 'Indian women'. Above: 'Ornamental cap of a chief', a skull cap of leather with woven beaded attachments, Choctaw? Above right: One of several sashes, belts or baldrics in the group of objects. This one is made of trade cloth with beadwork in the 'scroll' design, a possible reference to ball game sticks, Choctaw? Below right: A moccasin, of a construction common in eastern North America, made of one piece of buckskin with a centre front seam and turned down flaps, the heavy crimped seam is typical of the southeastern area. (Courtesy of the Marischal Museum, Marischal College, University of Aberdeen, Aberdeen, Scotland)

shell necklaces, and tattooing was common.

Decorative arts, such as those practised in other parts of North America, were not as fluorescent, but beadwork and thread embroidery were skilfully done by the Cherokee, Creek and Seminole, most notably on bandolier bags, coats and on men's belts and knee garters in the early 19th century. However, the isolation of the Florida Seminole during the 19th century resulted in the independent development of distinctive clothes. Here the use of cut and sewn patchwork quilted bands was developed, after the adoption of hand-cranked sewing machines, around 1895. Horizontal bands of quilting were first applied to men's 'long shirts', which were characterised by a front opening (suggesting a development from the European hunting coats or military coats popular amongst Creek and Cherokee men in the early 19th century). The 'big shirt', opened only to the waist, appeared about 1900, and later a short version allowing the use of trousers (pants) to become popular. The ingenious method of joining pieces of cotton cloth of contrasting colours was also adapted to women's skirts to form a dress, which became distinctly that of the Florida Seminole.

It is generally believed that the *Mikasuki* Seminole were the principal motivators of this new style of decoration. From about 1910 the style of quilting seems to indicate the date of manufacture: the bands gradually narrowed over time, with the complexity of designs constantly changed by expert seamstresses and sometimes influenced by white American commercial demands.

The Florida Seminole also retained the art of the preparation of buckskin hides, sold to white traders until recent times. Seminole and Creek men of the 19th century wore head turbans, silver gorgets, buckskin leggings, breechclouts, beaded baldrics or triangular-flap bandolier pouches and beaded or finger-woven woollen knee garters, all of which have long since fallen into disuse, but the ancient origins of some of these articles can be seen on the human figures engraved on the shells excavated from Spiro Mound, the Mississippian site in Oklahoma.

The Mississippi Choctaws have also been able to preserve a form of folk dress for special occasions, dances and fairs. Men's dress for such functions consists of a black felt hat or *Shapo* (from the French-Cajun *chapeau*) which is often decorated with ribbons

that hang loose over the brim at the back. Sometimes an eagle or turkey feather is attached, with vachis shaved away. Shirts are collarless cotton, invariably in a solid colour and with ribbon appliqué of contrasting colours along the sleeves' edges. Some men wear a silk scarf or a necklace of beads. A shoulder belt or baldric, single or in pairs, is often worn, and sometimes a belt with ribbons, perhaps simulating the old finger-woven sashes of the early 19th century. Commercial black slacks and shoes complete this outfit. Old moccasins were the classical eastern single-front-seam type of buckskin, with large angle or leg flaps. Catlin, the artist, sketched Choctaws in the 1830s in the 'hunting coat' – a cloth garment worn over the shirt, similar to those of the Creek and Seminole.

The Florida Seminole retained their distinctive dress of woven beaded sashes, long shirts with horizontal bands of contrasting cloth, and turbans during the 19th century. (Natural History Museum, Washington DC, USA)

Women wear German silver or beaded combs at the back of the crown and a beaded necklace in net or openwork. Dresses are full length, or nearly so, with a fitted top which has ruffles at the bottom, usually in one solid colour with appliqué work of contrasting colours on the bust, back and cuffs. Over the dress is worn a long white apron with ruffles, sometimes decorated with appliqué work. Silver earrings, bracelets and rings are widely used.

Decorative accessories such as baldrics and belts sometimes have beaded spiral or coiled snake designs (widespread in southeastern art right back to prehistoric times).

Hunting and food

Some classic scenes of Indian hunting were drawn by the Frenchman Jacques le Moyne of the *Timucua* of northern Florida during the 16th century. They show men disguising themselves with whole deerskins to approach within arrow-shot of their prey.

Mythology emphasised that the spirits of animals could be vengeful when killed if not placated by the hunter, although some hunters believed the allotted animal's life-span continued elsewhere after death.

An ancient hunting method was the use of cane blowguns – darts which could kill small animals up to 60 ft away. A few Eastern Cherokee descendants in North Carolina today can still demonstrate this hunting technique.

Deer was the most highly prized game for meat and hides; bears were hunted for their fat; and birds, particularly turkeys, were also much sought after. Meat was sometimes smoked over an open fire for winter storage. In Florida, alligators were killed by

Buckskin leggings (above) possibly southeastern c. 1830, part of a group of items supposed to have been obtained from Osceola, perhaps while imprisoned at Ft Moultrie, Charleston, South Carolina, and passed between commercial associates to Liverpool where they were deposited in a museum in 1878. Thread embroidery used here has been noted on several Cherokee coats. (National Museums & Galleries on Merseyside, Liverpool, UK)

Sash Seminole, below, c. 1835. A documented Seminole sash of cloth decorated with beadwork collected during the Second Seminole War 1835–42. (Private collection)

for winter storage; it would later be made into a gruel, baked, boiled or fried in bear's grease to make a flat cake. Coastal tribes prepared savoury stews of corn, meat and fish. (Fishing was common throughout the entire region.) The Cherokee, *Catawba* and *Chitmacha* produced split-cane baskets for the collection and storage of food.

Warriors and warfare

The Creek warrior fought almost naked; he wore just a breechclout, belt and moccasins, and his face and upper body were painted red and black. Individual warriors carried a bow and arrow or a gun and ammunition, and a knife and tomahawk or warclub through his belt. The warclub was about 2 ft long and described by white traders as 'gun-shaped', with an iron projection at the bend – suggesting a very similar weapon to that used by Indians of the North-eastern Woodlands. To complete his equipment he carried some parched corn, horse-ropes or halters and leather to repair moccasins.

A Creek war captain would announce his intention to invade a common enemy and recruit from among families who had lost people in enemy raids. In his winter round house his recruits drank consecrated herb and root decoctions to induce deities to guard and assist them against their enemies. Pledging support in sufficient numbers, once they had finished their fasting and purification, the warriors set off on raids which might take them away from their villages for weeks or even months.

The war captain or his assistant warrior or 'waiter' carried a holy ark or war bundle – usually made of thin sticks of wood and covered with hickory-splints – which contained consecrated materials of animal parts and sacred stones or divining crystals. This was never placed on the ground. The war party (usually 20–40 men), led by the captain and the leading warrior, moved silently, with a distance of a few steps between each warrior. Thus they proceeded while things promised them success; but if dreams portended ill, they might return home. On the trail, warriors drank little (water was carried in a hollowed cane, corked at both ends), often mortifying their bodies to gain divine favour; they rarely rested against a tree, sat in the shade, or killed animals for food. (They were particularly wary of killing animals that were regarded highly for their

Pouch and belt of red trade cloth (c. 1850). The pouch has a triangular flap and is decorated in typical Seminole beadwork. Attributed to Billy Bowlegs the Seminole chief during the Third Seminole War in Florida 1855–58. (National History Museum, Smithsonian Institution, Washington DC, USA photograph M.G. Johnson)

ramming a 10 ft pole down the throat of the beast and killing it with arrows and clubs. Coastal tribes ate clams, crayfish and crabs.

Indian corn (maize) was known to most southwestern Indians (except the *Calusa*), and they sometimes harvested two crops of corn each year along with beans and squash. The knowledge of corn cultivation and that of beans, squash and chilli had spread through Mexico's central valley and coastal regions, and reached northwards, into the Mississippi and Ohio river valleys, by the time of the late Adenas and early Hopewells. Maize agriculture reached its zenith among the later Mississippians, but remained important to their heirs, the southeastern tribes. The autumn corn harvest was dried spiritual value, such as bear or deer, in case they angered the animals' deities.)

When close to enemy villages or hunting grounds, they proceeded with great caution. If a small war party, they might crawl during daylight, and climb trees or gain high ground to discover the smoke of fires. When they crossed through open areas in the woods, some warriors would cover their comrades from behind trees. To remain undetected they would take oblique courses, or walk on trees which had blown down to conceal their tracks and avoid pursuit. When enemies encountered each other, they spoke loud insults and emitted shrill war-cries and death-whoops as they pursued each other from tree to tree. Each party desperately tried to save their dead and wounded from being scalped (usually performed by slashing round the top of the skull with a scalping knife and stripping off the scalp). The vanquished party quickly disappeared from the fray by taking to the swampy thickets, but speedy pursuers often took captives, who would later be tied to a stake and might be tortured by women on return to the victors' village. Enemy scalps were fixed to the tops of houses or carried on branches of the evergreen pines until they had appeased the ghosts of the victors' own dead. Sometimes young enemy captives might be adopted.

Among the Creeks, Seminoles and Cherokee, warlike functions, declaration of war judgement on captives, and elections of war chiefs took place in towns or by clans designated for these purposes; in contrast there were some towns where peace treaties were negotiated and where it was forbidden to shed human blood. Among the Creeks the term 'Red Sticks' has often been applied to warriors from the most noted towns controlled by the war clans such as the *Atasi* of the Upper Creeks and the *Kawita (Coweta)* of the Lower Creeks. (The *Mikasuki* produced most warriors among the Seminole.) The symbol of war and a rallying point for the warriors was a red-painted pole in the public square – hence 'Red Sticks'. However, a more probable derivation was from the method of recording the number of days a war party was on the trail by counting sticks. Warriors left for war with parched corn cakes as provisions and equipped with a warclub, or later a metal tomahawk, bow and arrow, spear, sling and knife. In ancient times wooden or leather shields, breast pieces and arm bracelets afforded some protection. When a successful war party returned, a purification ritual was necessary before a victory dance could be held. The rituals for peace, menstruation, purification and the great agricultural festivals were held by the white clans or in towns designated white towns.

Intertribal wars and internal factional disputes were common. McIntosh, a Lower Creek mixed-blood from Coweta, was leader of the pro-American

An expertly tailored coat (c. 1850) patterned from Euro-American broad-caped hunting and military coats. It closely resembles three known Cherokee coats in US collections with thread embroidery in floral designs. (By kind permission of Birmingham Museum & Art Gallery, UK)

A fine example of Seminole art in beadwork decoration on this cloth bandolier with a triangular flap (c. 1820). Some of the beads are gold-plated. (John W. Painter Collection, Ohio) southeast bandolier bags were perhaps derived from European military shot pouches and developed into prestigious and baroque forms, similar to those more commonly associated with the Northern Woodland Indians. By the early 19th century they served as ethnic symbols rather than usable accessories of the backwoodsmen, Indian or white, while on the trail or hunting. Some surviving early 19th-century Creek and Seminole bandoliers are characterised by the triangular flap and beadwork of figurative and abstract designs, perhaps of ancient origin, with symbolic and esoteric meanings. A possible Afro-American influence may also be present.

tough team game – similar to lacrosse, except that two small sticks were used instead of the one in lacrosse. The game was played between two teams, with ten or more men per side, originally from different villages. It was played with a small leather ball, and goal-posts about 150 yds apart. Players with appropriately painted faces and bodies advanced into the field from opposite directions, yelling defiance, and met in the centre of the field facing each other. A medicine man tossed the ball between the players, who then attempted to catch it between their sticks. Players then blocked their opponents or cleared a way towards the goal. Points were counted by successfully getting the ball through the goal, and the first team making 12 scores was the winner. The ball game was excellent training for war: it required speed, agility, cunning and strength – and sometimes ended in death. The game is still played by Creeks, Seminoles and Choctaws.

Another men's game was 'Chunkey', played with a stone disc and a pole. The disc was rolled ahead and the object of the game was to throw the wooden pole as close as possible to the spot where they expected the disc to fall. This game is extremely old, and was played on pitches especially prepared for the purpose in larger villages – called 'Chunkey yards' by white traders.

Choctaw and Lower Mississippi tribal history

French interest in the South began after the expedition of Marquette and Jolliet through the Illinois country and down the Mississippi River. In 1682 La Salle began to expand his Great Lakes Indian commerce from Fort Frontenac into the Mississippi Valley. He led a party to the mouth of the Mississippi River and established contact with the *Quapaw*, *Taensa* and *Natchez*. La Salle's role in the commercial drive into the Lower Mississippi Valley ended with his assassination in 1687 after a struggle to save his Texas colony, but the explorer Tonti sustained the trade of bison and beaver hides from the area. In 1698 Spain established a permanent garrison at Pensacola Bay (Florida), but the most aggressive challenge to the French control of the Lower Mississippi region originated from the British of the Carolinas. In 1699 Pierre le Moyne D'Iberville established the French post at Biloxi, in close vicinity of the *Biloxi*, *Pascagoula* and *Moctobi* tribes. Despite the

faction amongst the Creeks in the Creek war of 1812–14, and was later killed by rival chief Menawa's warriors; and Major John Ridge, who held a similar pro-American position among the Cherokee, was murdered along with members of his family and supporters by other Cherokee shortly after they had been moved to Indian Territory.

Indian ball game

Cherokee, Creek, Seminole and Choctaw played a

diplomatic efforts of D'Iberville and his brother De Bienville, the hostility between Great Britain and France destabilised Indian tribal relationships. Chickasaws under British influence remained at war with the Choctaws, and the *Alabamas* continued to raid French-allied Indian towns and Spanish missions in Florida. Among the Indians of the lower Red River, the *Bayogoulas* and *Chitimachas* probably suffered the worst hardships under French colonisation. The French missionary Father Saint-Cosme was killed by *Chitimachas* after they had been attacked by Indians in French interest in 1706. The *Chitimacha* village on Bayou La Fourche was destroyed by the French in retaliation. Generally the Choctaws formed a relationship with the French similar to that of the Iroquois with the British in New York, and were treated as a separate nation (if inferior) by the whites. They occasionally broke ranks and allied themselves to British traders, thus ensuring a supply of gifts from both the British and French as evidence of friendship and tribute for the use of their lands. If gifts stopped, an act of aggression was presumed by the Indians, similar to that which happened in the Ohio country in Pontiac's rebellion of 1763.

The Yamasee war in the Carolinas disrupted British trade with the interior tribes, allowing the French to build Fort Toulouse, near the junction of the Coosa and Tallapoosa rivers in 1717, and bring the Upper Creeks within French commercial interests; Fort Rosalie had been built among the Natchez the previous year. Fort St. Pierre, on the Yazoo River, and posts amongst the *Kadohadacho* and other Caddoan groups on the Red River completed the contour of French commercial trade, which consisted largely of the exchange of deer hides for European products. In 1729 the Natchez rose in rebellion against the French and attacked Fort Rosalie, but were forced to abandon their villages after combined attacks by French and Choctaws. Many Natchez were later sold into slavery in Santo Domingo; some sought refuge amongst the Chickasaw, and other refugees were allowed to settle in South Carolina and joined the Cherokee.

The French never defeated the Chickasaw, however. The latter resisted all the incursions by the French and their Choctaw allies into their territory; but the French often captured Chickasaws, and offered bounty for Chickasaw scalps. In 1746 the

Choctaw, themselves now divided in their relationship with the French, plunged into civil war, and their western towns openly rebelled against German and French settlements. Pro-French Choctaws presented scalps of many of their own warriors to the officials at Mobile, and the two remaining hostile Choctaw towns surrendered in 1750. In all American colonies, French, British or Spanish officials patronised the chiefs who best served their interests; this intensified factionalism. Native ceremonies, such as the Calumet ritual designed to reaffirm alliances, were encouraged, to ensure services from Indian leaders. Under the leadership of Abilamon Mingo, the Choctaws resumed regular trade with the French and produced more deerskins for exportation than any other tribe in the area. The remains of the smaller tribes closer to French settlements became enclaves of diminished tribal groups drawn into the economy of colonists as traders, servants and labourers – some even added to the numbers of African-American slaves in white households and plantations.

Mississippi Choctaw man in dance dress c. 1908. Note the beaded sashes and belt with possible ball game and other motifs.

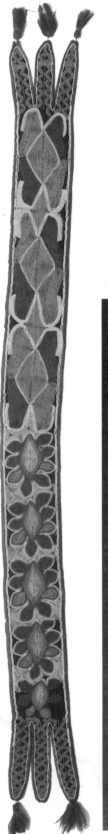

Left: Sash or strap from a bandolier bag. Reported to have belonged to Osceola, the famous Seminole hero. The sash is southeastern in style (Creek-Seminole). (National Museums & Galleries on Merseyside, Liverpool, UK)

Below left: Belt or baldric, probably Choctaw. Cloth with beadwork in scroll design (c. 1825), probably the ancient snake or serpent designs of tribal mythology. Similar examples have survived from the Cherokee. (The Manchester Museum, UK)

Above: Alabama (Creek) belt c. 1880. Red cloth with beadwork in cross and circle designs probably representing sticks and ball of the native ball game. (National History Museum, Smithsonian Institution, Washington DC, USA photograph M.G. Johnson)

With the transfer of French territory to the British in 1763, after the Treaty of Paris, lands east of the Mississippi above Lake Pontchartrain became British, and the Spanish took control of Louisiana. Indians responded resourcefully to the political diversity of the region, and new officials accepted their fans, smoked their pipes and distributed peace medals. However, the non-native population was now increasing, with Acadians, English, Creoles, Canary Islanders and, after the American Revolution, Anglo-Americans.

While some Choctaws continued traditional farming methods of burning the underbrush for planting corn, beans, pumpkins, melons and sunflowers, increasing numbers adopted Euro-American material culture, farming methods, dress and weapons; eventually many Indians abandoned their native lifestyle for that of the white frontier people. In 1805 Chief Pushmataha signed the Treaty of Mount Dexter with the United States. This began the cession of lands which ultimately led to a treaty in 1830 by which the Choctaw largely moved to Indian Territory, to become one of the 'Five Civilized Tribes'; their political and economic life thenceforth was led by mixed-blood leaders such as Greenwood Le Flore. Chickasaw friendship with the British was transferred to the Americans after the Revolution, and few disputes arose with the new US government. Following a series of treaties between 1805 and 1832 they too yielded their lands east of the Mississippi River for lands in Indian Territory, where their own national government was established, similar to that of the Choctaws. The smaller tribes of the area intermixed with the Creoles or joined the larger tribes, leaving few Indians in the Lower Mississippi area by 1840 – their lands were now in the hands of the white man. The ancient animal paths, Indian trails that linked villages, warpaths, village sites, cemeteries and mounds had been separated from the native people and passed to the newcomers for exploitation.

Cherokee history

It was not until 1654 that the English from Virginia came into contact with the Cherokee. The Virginian Indians, the *Powhatans*, were being constantly harassed, and joined the English in a retaliatory expedition in 1658. In 1670 the German explorer John Lederer followed the trail of the Virginian traders to the southern tribes, and the same year saw the establishment of the colony of South Carolina and the beginning of formal treaties between that colony and the Cherokee. In 1691 colonists murdered several of the tribe, and in 1693 Cherokee chiefs went to Charleston to ask for aid against the *Catawba* and *Shawnee*. Later, in 1705, they complained to Governor Moore about the assaults by whites on their towns.

In the Tuscarora War, 1711–13, the Cherokees took an active, but not overly important, role in aiding the English against their old enemies: with the South Carolina volunteers over 1,000 Indians, including 200 Cherokee, overran the *Tuscarora*, many of whose number were sold into slavery or fled north to join their kinsmen, the Iroquois. Having settled old scores with the *Tuscarora*, the Cherokee, in concert with many tribes – from Cape Fear in the north to the Chattahoochee River in the south – rose against the English in the so-called Yamasee War of 1715.

The Cherokees claimed the uprising was, at least in part, due to the misconduct of some English traders and the enslavement of many Indian people. It was a conspiracy, similar to that of the *Powhatans* under Opechancaough in Virginia, to extirpate all whites. The Yamasee, at this time the largest tribe in close contact with the colony of South Carolina, launched a series of raids against the colony's settlements. The colonists soon rallied, under Governor Craven, and crushed the beleaguered Yamasee,

whose remnants abandoned the country for Florida or joined the Creeks. The English then made short work of the smaller coastal tribes, and the Cherokee were soon glad to sue for peace.

By this time the French had established settlements at Biloxi Bay, Mississippi, in 1699, built Fort Toulouse on the Coosa River, near present-day Montgomery, Alabama, and were extending their influence to the surrounding Creek tribes. From this time, until French withdrawal from the American colonies in 1763, the area was a stage for the struggle for colonial supremacy between France and Britain. The Chickasaw, whose territory bordered the Mississippi and French domain, controlled French advances northwards, and the British kept them well supplied with guns and ammunition. In 1730 the Cherokee were visited by Sir Alexander Cuming, in response to grievances which saw them ready to join the Creeks against the English. Several Cherokee chiefs visited London and reaffirmed their British alliance. The culture of the interior tribes was now being much affected by the adoption of European goods – horses, cattle and pigs – but the slave ships brought with them smallpox in 1738, and the Cherokee lost many (some by suicide) in the resulting ravages. They were often at war: with surrounding tribes, Chickasaw and Shawnee; with the Iroquois in the north; and in the war with the Creeks for possession of upper Georgia which continued on and off. (The Creeks, although willing to be at peace with the English, were determined to keep the war with their traditional enemies, the Cherokee.)

The English had encroached so much on Cherokee territory by the outbreak of the French and Indian War, in 1754, that even military posts were in Cherokee territory: Fort Loudoun had been built on the Little Tennessee River and Fort Prince George on the Savannah. The Cherokee were by no means fully committed to the British cause in the coming conflict. Lawless officers from Fort Prince George committed outrages in neighbouring Indian villages while warriors were away, which began a series of events which led to all-out war – the Cherokee and other tribes against the British. Led by Ononostota, they descended upon frontier settlements in the Carolinas and laid siege to Fort Loudoun, in 1760, which surrendered that same year. The captives were ransomed, but one officer, Captain John Stuart, es-

Indian hunting. An Indian method of hunting, dressed in deer skins approaching prey. Note the bow and cane quiver. Diorama. (Jamestown Settlement Museum, Williamsburg, Virginia, USA, photograph M.G. Johnson)

caped and was led through the wilderness by a friendly Cherokee and delivered safely to friends in Virginia. Stuart later became the British Superintendent for the southern tribes.

Colonel Grant invaded Cherokee country in 1761 with an army of 2,600, including Chickasaw auxiliaries, and destroyed many towns and cornfields. On the conclusion of peace between France and Great Britain in 1763, Stuart and the governors of Virginia, North Carolina, South Carolina and Georgia met at Augusta, and a peace treaty was concluded with the Cherokee in November. (Three Cherokee chiefs had visited London the previous year in an attempt to cément relations.)

The period between the end of the French and Indian War and the American Revolution was notable for the number of cessions by the Indians in a fruitless endeavour to fix permanent boundaries between themselves and advancing white settlements. The territory originally claimed by the Cherokee extended north to the Ohio River, but by the time of the Revolution it had been reduced to no more than half of their former domain.

At the time of the Cherokee removal in 1838, only a core area around the junction of the states of Alabama, Georgia and Tennessee remained in Indian hands. Just before the outbreak of the Revolution, the botanist William Bartram made an extended tour of Cherokee country. He left a pleasant account of Indian life, and noted their friendly disposition. At the outset of the Revolution, the tribes ranged on the British side, as they appeared to the native peoples to be the sole representatives of authority against encroachment by American frontier settlers. Licensed British traders, particularly Scottish and Irish, were resident in every Indian tribe of the area and many had intermarried and raised families. They were encouraged in their resolve against the Americans with promises of plunder from the settlements. In 1776 the Americans equipped four expeditions to enter Cherokee territory simultaneously from as many different directions. Those led by Griffith Rutherford, of Irish origin, and William Christian rendered crushing blows to Cherokee towns and wasted their cornfields. Women were shot down, and cattle and horses killed, until the Cherokee were compelled to sue for peace.

The Cherokee concluded their first treaty with the new US in 1785, which resulted in most of their lands east of the Blue Ridge being given over to whites, but war resumed in 1792 and Cherokees from the Hiwassee and Chickamauga bands, under a mixed-blood leader, John Watts, together with some Creeks, raided new American settlements in Tennessee. Peace was restored in 1794. From then till their removal west, in 1838, the Cherokee made considerable steps towards American assimilation, and the invention of Sequoya's alphabet had an immediate effect on their institutions. The mixed-bloods had translated the Bible, published a newspaper, founded

Adena and Hopewell
1: Adena priest, c. 500–200 BC
2: Hopewell priest, c. 300–AD 500
3: Hopewell woman, c. AD 500
4: Hopewell man, c. AD 300
5: Hopewell platform pipes, c. 100 BC–AD 400

1

2

3   5   4   A

Mississippian
1: Chunkey player, c. 1200–1500
2: Chunkey player
3: Birdman dancer, c. 1200–1500
4: Mississippian priest, c. 1200–1500

B

Mississippian and the 16th century
1: Spiro warrior in armour, c. 1250
2: Mississipian woman from Tennessee, c. 1250
3: Spiro man, c. 1200–1350
4: Timucua man, c. 1564
5: Timucuan woman, c. 1564
6: Key Marco - wooden sculptures, c. 900–1400

C

Southern Indians visit London, 1734
1: Tomochichi's wife
2: Tomochichi

D

18th century
1: Cherokee man, c. 1790
2: Koasati-Creek man, c. 1790
3: Tunica chief, c. 1735
4: Atakapa warrior, c. 1735

E

Seminole warriors of the
2nd Seminole War, 1835-42
1: Seminole warrior, c. 1836
2: Seminole warrior, c. 1836
3: Black Seminole guide, c. 1836
4: Seminole warrior, c. 1836

19th century
1: Creek chief, c. 1826
2: Eastern Cherokee Booger dancers, c. 1900
3: Western Cherokee capitol building
4: Cherokee ball-game player, c. 1890
5: Stand Watie

20th century
1: Oklahoma-Creek girl, c. 1950
2: Mississippian-Choctaw man, c. 1910
3: Mississippian-Choctaw woman, c. 1980
4: Florida-Seminole woman and child, c. 1915

H

schools, and even made plans for a museum and national library at their capital, New Echota. They had become the leading families of the nation. Sequoya (George Guess) was of German origin; the Doughertys, Galpins and Adairs Irish; and the Ross, Vann and McIntosh families Scottish.

This period before removal saw great cultural changes and continual political pressure for removal by the Government, which all but wore out their resolve. Their leader, John Ross, continued the political fight, but another prominent mixed-blood family, the Ridges, and their allies were now prepared to negotiate for removal. (Some Cherokee bands had already given up the cause to remain in their ancient homelands; they had settled in Arkansas and Missouri and become known as the 'Old Settlers'.) Divided now into two factions, one headed by Major John Ridge who were now prepared for removal and the National Party, headed by John Ross, they began negotiations in 1835 that ended with the Treaty of New Echota. This ceded to the US the whole of the remaining Cherokee territory east of the Mississippi River for five million dollars, in return for new lands in the west. Removal took place in

Tahchee or a Dutch, Cherokee chief who removed west long before the main body of the tribe in order to lead a lifestyle free of white influences. (From a lithograph published by McKenney & Hall 1836–44.)

1838. It was evident that removal could only be accomplished by force, and General Winfield Scott was appointed to enforce a tragedy hardly surpassed in American history. Nearly 17,000 Cherokee were gathered into stockades by troops, put on steamers and transported down the Tennessee and Ohio rivers to the farther side of the Mississippi. Their journey into Indian Territory (now the State of Oklahoma) was continued by land. It is difficult to estimate the number of people who died as a result of the removal. Those removed under John Ross lost over 1,600 on the journey; perhaps 4,000 Cherokee died on this the 'Trail of Tears'. Within a few months of arriving in

Creek man's coat c. 1820. The coat is of velvet and cloth with a shawl-like collar at the back, and appears to have been derived from English and American hunting or military coats of the 18th century adopted by Appalachian frontiersmen and Indians. Several chiefs and tribal diplomats visiting Washington were painted by artists in the 1820s and 30s wearing such coats. This example has quilting around the lower body and the sleeves have been modified by adding beaded garters usually worn with leggings. (From the permanent collection of the Montclair Art Museum, Montclair, New Jersey, USA)

SE-QUO-YAH.
INVENTOR OF THE CHEROKEE ALPHABET

Sequoya, the Cherokee who invented the syllabary which allowed many Cherokee to become literate. Spent later years searching for lost bands of his people in the west. (Lithograph published by McKenney and Hall 1836–44)

their independence, and Samuel Houston concluded a formal treaty with these Cherokee. However, in 1838 Houston was succeeded by Lamar, who announced his intention to expel every Indian tribe from Texas. The Texas Cherokee and their confederates, splinters of many eastern tribes, were attacked and defeated by Texan troops under General Douglas in 1839. As a result most Cherokee rejoined their kinsmen in Indian Territory; those who did not gradually drifted down to Mexico where several hundred settled around Guadalajara and Lake Chapala. Sequoya, the mixed-blood who devised the syllabary which bears his name, spent much of his later life trying to find some of the 'lost' bands of Cherokee in the west. He died in Mexico in 1843.

Sequoya, whose father was a German, was born about 1760 and lived as a boy near Fort Loudoun. He became a good silverworker, hunter and trader, but an accident rendered him a cripple for life. As a consequence, he turned to his more contemplative disposition and evolved the syllabary of 86 alphabetical characters which rendered the Cherokee a literate people within a decade or so.

The Cherokee nation in Indian Territory reorganised with a seat of government at Tahlequah, though divided between the old Ridge and Ross factions, and also by blood. The full-bloods, perhaps one third of the population, took refuge in the hill districts, while the mixed-bloods occupied the low grounds and later the railroad towns. Native language, allegiances and traditions faded quickly among the prosperous prominent families whose lifestyle resembled that of white Southerners – including the ownership of black slaves. At the outbreak of the Civil War in 1861, as slave owner; the Cherokee sympathised with the Confederacy. The Ross faction were for neutrality, but two Cherokee regiments were raised for Confederate service under Stand Watie and Colonel Drew. As a result, their lands were ruined by guerilla warfare, schools were broken up, flocks and herds slaughtered and orchards destroyed. Their whole country was in ashes. By 1898 the western Cherokee nation had ceded unoccupied lands to the USA. They numbered 34,461, including 26,500 by blood; the rest were negro freed men, intermarried whites and other intermarried or incorporated Indians of other tribes. Their descendants are in Oklahoma still.

their new lands many members of the Ridge family and Elias Boudinot had been murdered by adherents of the National Party led by John Ross. Not all Cherokees joined their kinsmen in Indian Territory: chief Tahchee (Dutch) crossed into Texas and joined a colony already there under a chief called 'The Bowl'.

The first permanent Cherokee settlement beyond the Mississippi River was a direct result of the hostilities of 1794, and later, after the treaty of June 1817 by which the Cherokees ceded two considerable tracts, the first in Georgia and the other in Tennessee, a further Cherokee migration to Arkansas took place. The majority of those who voluntarily removed desired to re-establish the old Indian life. By 1828 a number had crossed into Texas, then under Mexican jurisdiction; by 1836 the Texans had gained

A number of Cherokee escaped removal by fleeing to the Great Smoky Mountains or to the headwaters of the Oconaluftee River and in part, due to the efforts of a trader, William Thomas, were allowed to remain in their homelands thereafter. The Eastern band of the Cherokee and their descendants still remain on the Qualla Reservation in western North Carolina.

The Creek war of 1812–14

A number of people who rose to distinction among the Creek were descendants of adventurers from Europe. They were at first traders, obtaining pelts in exchange for goods the Indians required – cloth, guns, metal tomahawks and kettles – and they also introduced black slaves. They married into all the major southern interior tribes, becoming emancipated and incorporated within the blood lines of leading families, thus producing, within a generation, principal chiefs of mixed descent. Such a man, born about 1780, became known to whites as William Weatherford. He was a son of Charles Weatherford, a Scottish trader, and his mother was the sister of Alexander McGillivray, another prominent and shrewd mixed-blood chief. Despite his European genealogy, he was essentially Creek by culture – a fine athlete, ball player and horseman. He was influenced by the visit to the Creeks of Tecumseh the Shawnee in 1811, who was urging the southern tribes to rebel against the Americans and to join his confederacy in the North in a general uprising. The Americans viewed Tecumseh as an agent of the British in the approaching war of 1812 and he did ultimately join with the British after the collapse of his cause at Tippecanoe, in 1811.

Weatherford, with other chiefs, began plans for a war against the white settlers in Alabama, but the Creeks were split in their desire for war, and a number of internal disputes between the white (peace towns) and the red (war towns) led to near civil war within the nation. This alarmed both the settlers and some of the acculturated and slave-owning mixed-bloods, some of whom took refuge at Fort Mims, located in southern Alabama almost at the junction of the Alabama and Tombigbee rivers. Although Weatherford wavered in his resolve for war (his affection for families who had taken refuge at Fort Mims and the exposed position of his own

Yoholo-Micco, a Creek chief 1790–1838. After a painting by Henry Inman, *a copy of a painting by Charles Bird King c. 1831–33.*

family and livestock caused him to reconsider), he finally threw himself into battle.

Fort Mims, constructed by Samuel Mims and his neighbours, had a total of 550 people inside and in its vicinity, including 245 military and militia. Several reports of Indians near the fort went unheeded, and the warriors rushed the main gates which had been opened for repair, some reports say, or jammed open with sand. The battle, on 30 August 1813, was one of the most bloody in American frontier history. Over 500 whites and blacks perished. About 20 occupants of the fort succeeded in chopping a hole through the outer picketing and escaped.

The news of Fort Mims alarmed the entire white population on the Creek frontier, and the Government despatched General Andrew Jackson southward with 3,000 Tennessee volunteers and regulars, reinforced by 500 Cherokees, mostly recruited by

Major Ridge and led by Chief Junaluska and some American Creeks under McIntosh (later killed by his own people). They plundered through Creek towns until, in March 1814, they confronted Weatherford's (Red Eagle's) terrified anti-American Creeks concentrated on a sort of peninsula called Horseshoe – a bend in the Tallapoosa River enclosing a hundred acres of ground. Across this narrow place the Creeks had constructed a strong wooden fortification, designed to resist even artillery-fire. Within this enclosure, houses were further protected by embankments of earth. Reinforced with fresh recruits from Tennessee, Jackson's army hurled themselves against the fortification, and despite heavy losses overwhelmed the Creeks. There were 557 dead warriors found in the compound, and uncounted numbers were killed in the river, trying to make their escape. Warchief Menawa escaped, but Weatherford surren-

A romantic 19th-century drawing of the surrender of the mixed-blood Creek leader William Weatherford (also known as Red Eagle) to General Andrew Jackson following the Battle of Horseshoe Bend in 1814. Jackson, instead of punishing the Indian leader, gave him protection and liberty, allowing him to return to his plantation, family, friends and slaves in Monroe County, Alabama. Several of his children married whites. He died in 1824. (Sketch by unknown artist)

dered by walking into Jackson's camp. Legend has it that Jackson, recognising a patriot, instead of punishment offered Weatherford protection. He was released on his word to use his influence to maintain peace – which he did. He lived with his wives, children and slaves in Monroe County, Alabama, until his death in 1824. The Creeks were ultimately forced to remove to new lands in Indian Territory, now Oklahoma, where their descendants remain.

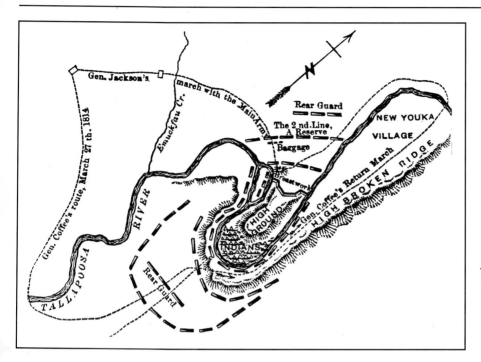

Plan of the battle of Horseshoe Bend 1814. Anti-American Creeks led by Weatherford and Menawa made a stand against the Americans under Andrew Jackson at a fortified position in a bend of the Tallapoosa River, Alabama, but were badly defeated, effectively ending their resistance to American settlement of their lands.

The Seminole wars

The Seminoles, whose history is so firmly associated with Florida, were not native to the state. They are descended from parts of tribes who, from time to time, moved south to replace near extinct groups in the northern part of the state. The earliest immigrants were from the Lower Creek towns of Georgia, particularly the *Oconee* and *Mikasuki*, from the Hitchiti-speaking groups who enslaved other refugee groups from the north, the Yamasee and Yuchi. By 1750 there was a sizeable population, which had probably absorbed the few remaining *Timucua* and *Calusa* Indians – the original natives of Florida. Later, true Creeks, Muskogee speakers from the Upper Creek towns, added to the growing Seminole

William McIntosh was a mixed-blood chief of the Lower Creeks; son of a Scottish trader and a Creek woman, who had become leader of the pro-American faction of his people by the time of the British-American conflict of 1812. His followers aided the Americans against hostile Creeks at Atasi in 1813 and Horseshoe Bend in 1814. He and his followers acquiesced in the sale of lands to the Americans in 1823 and were sentenced to death by other Creeks as a consequence. Menawa's warriors killed him at his house on 1 May 1825 for 'selling the graves of their ancestors'. (Photograph courtesy of the Alabama Department of Archives and History, Montgomery, Alabama, USA)

37

Yahd-Hajd or The Madwolf, a Creek chief who had visited Washington in 1826 but later emigrated to Florida, becoming a Seminole leader and part of the deputation sent west after the Treaty of Payne's Landing, 1832, to examine their proposed new homeland. He later opposed removal and was killed during the Seminole War in 1836. (Lithograph published by McKenney and Hall 1836–44 from a painting by C.B. King in 1826)

Mick-e-no-pah (Micanopy), a Seminole chief during the Second Seminole War; painted by George Catlin while

Micanopy was imprisoned with Osceola at Ft Moultrie, South Carolina, in 1838.

Right: Seminole country.

population. In 1763 Spain lost Florida to England, and it remained in British hands until 1783; following the Revolutionary War it again became a Spanish possession. However, border clashes were frequent, as black slaves were offered freedom and sanctuary by the Seminoles and white plantation owners crossed into Florida to recapture their human chattels. As Federal law prohibited further importation of slaves from Africa, the recapture of black fugitives who formed separate but politically integrated Seminole towns became of paramount importance to the southern plantation economy.

In 1812 the US invaded Spanish Florida. The soldiers were forced to retreat, but Chief King Payne, leader of the Seminole since the death of his uncle Chief Secoffee in 1785, a pro-British chief, was killed. Payne was succeeded by his younger brother Micanopy. Following the Creek war of 1812–14 more Creek refugees fled to Florida and the Seminole population doubled. Between 1816 and 1818 Federal forces made several attacks on Seminole and Black-Seminole towns. This, known as the First Seminole War, began a long series of bitter struggles, which intensified after the transfer of Florida to the USA in

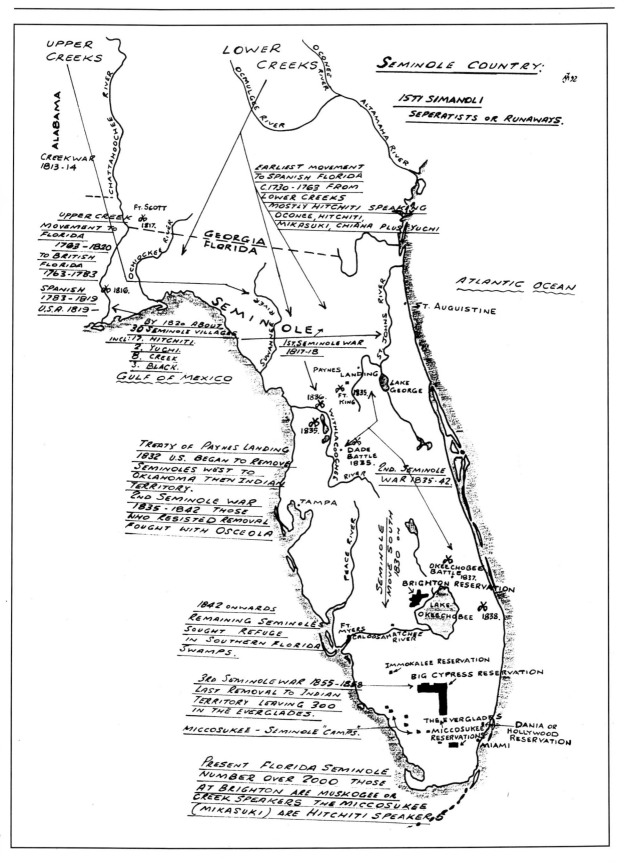

UPPER CREEKS

LOWER CREEKS

SEMINOLE COUNTRY.

1571 SIMANOLI
SEPERATISTS OR RUNAWAYS.

ALABAMA

CREEK WAR 1813-14

OCMULGEE RIVER

OCONEE RIVER

ALTAMAHA RIVER

CHATTAHOOCHEE RIVER

FT. SCOTT 1817.

EARLIEST MOVEMENT TO SPANISH FLORIDA C.1730-1763 FROM LOWER CREEKS MOSTLY HITCHITI SPEAKING OCONEE, HITCHITI, MIKASUKI, CHIAHA PLUS YUCHI

UPPER CREEK MOVEMENT TO FLORIDA 1763-1820
TO BRITISH FLORIDA 1763-1783
SPANISH 1783-1819
U.S.A. 1819-

OCHLOCKEE RIVER

1816.

GEORGIA
FLORIDA

ATLANTIC OCEAN

ST. AUGUSTINE

SEMINOLE

BY 1820 ABOUT 30 SEMINOLE VILLAGES INCL: 17. HITCHITI.
2. YUCHI.
8. CREEK.
3. BLACK.
GULF OF MEXICO

SUWANEE RIVER

ST. JOHNS RIVER

1ST. SEMINOLE WAR 1817-18

PAYNES LANDING

1836.

FT. KING

1835.

LAKE GEORGE

1835.

WITHLACOOCHEE RIVER

TREATY OF PAYNES LANDING 1832 U.S. BEGAN TO REMOVE SEMINOLES WEST TO OKLAHOMA THEN INDIAN TERRITORY.
2ND SEMINOLE WAR 1835-1842 THOSE WHO RESISTED REMOVAL FOUGHT WITH OSCEOLA

DADE BATTLE 1835.

2ND. SEMINOLE WAR 1835-42.

TAMPA

PEACE RIVER

SEMINOLE MOVE SOUTH 1830 on

OKEECHOBEE BATTLE 1837.
BRIGHTON RESERVATION

1842 ONWARDS REMAINING SEMINOLES SOUGHT REFUGE IN SOUTHERN FLORIDA SWAMPS.

FT. MYERS
CALOOSAHATCHEE RIVER

LAKE OKEECHOBEE 1838.

3RD SEMINOLE WAR 1855-1858 LAST REMOVAL TO INDIAN TERRITORY LEAVING 300 IN THE EVERGLADES.

MICCOSUKEE - SEMINOLE "CAMPS."

IMMOKALEE RESERVATION
BIG CYPRESS RESERVATION

THE EVERGLADES
MICCOSUKEE RESERVATIONS

DANIA OR HOLLYWOOD RESERVATION

MIAMI

PRESENT FLORIDA SEMINOLE NUMBER OVER 2000 THOSE AT BRIGHTON ARE MUSKOGEE OR CREEK SPEAKERS THE MICCOSUKEE (MIKASUKI) ARE HITCHITI SPEAKERS.

1819, when General (then Governor) Andrew Jackson informed the Seminole chiefs that they would have to move all their people to one central area of the territory. By the time Jackson became President, in 1829, his plan to remove all Indians remaining east of the Mississippi to Indian Territory (now Oklahoma) was gaining support; it became a reality when he signed the Indian Removal Act in 1830.

In 1832 the Seminole leaders met Government officials at Payne's Landing, on the Oklawaha River near Silver Springs, Florida. Here it was agreed to send a party of chiefs west to inspect the proposed new Seminole lands. John Blunt, Charley Emathla, Jumper and Black Dirt made the long journey in 1833 and were persuaded to sign a document apparently promising removal of all Seminoles from Florida; they were given until 1836 to prepare for removal. When the chiefs returned from Indian Territory, confusion arose, as some chiefs swore they had never signed the treaty. While several of the older chiefs, such as Micanopy, agreed to move, the Blacks among the Seminole refused to follow their masters into exile. It was at this time Osceola (Assi Yahola), of Upper Creek and white descent, is first noted, as the leader of a war party against Charley Emathla, a strong supporter of removal. Thus began the Second Seminole War (1835–42), the most costly Indian campaign ever fought by the United States Army. Over 1,500 soldiers were killed along with many civilians, in a tragic conflict which saw a total of 4,420 Seminoles captured or surrendered and deported to Indian Territory. Initially the Seminoles had success: Thompson, the agent urging removal, was killed during an engagement with a band of *Mikasukis* led by Osceola, and an army detachment led by Major Francis Dade was ambushed and almost wiped out by a party of warriors led by Micanopy, Jumper and Alligator. The struggle became a guerilla campaign, with a few hundred Seminoles using the forest and swamps as hiding places against increasingly frustrated military commanders. Under a flag of truce, Osceola was seized by direction of General Thomas Jesup, who spent much of the rest of his life trying to justify his action. Osceola's band were taken first to St Augustine and Fort Marion but were later transferred to Fort Moultrie, South Carolina, where Osceola died, probably of malaria, on 30 January

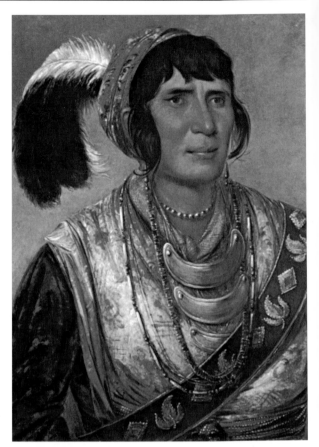

Osceola 'Black drink crier' c. 1803–38, Seminole leader during the Second Seminole War. He died a prisoner at Ft Moultrie, Charleston, in January 1838, a few days after the artist George Catlin painted his portrait. He was born of Creek parents, although his paternal grandfather was a Scotsman and he was sometimes also known as Powell, the name of his mother's white second husband after the death of his own father. He moved to Florida following the Creek War (1812–14) and gained a formidable reputation during the Seminoles' memorable struggle with the Americans. He is a hero to modern Florida Seminoles, and several families perpetuate his name.

1838. With him were Micanopy, Philip, Coa Hadjo, Cloud, 116 warriors and 82 women and children, including his own family (although two children may have remained in Florida). By 1842 perhaps only 500 Seminoles were left in Florida, mostly restricted to the lower half of the peninsula.

The Third Seminole War broke out in 1855 between a few Seminole warriors under Billy Bowlegs, around Lake Okeechobee and in the depths of the Everglades. From this group of independent

Three members of Billy Bowlegs' band, possibly drawn from photographs taken in 1858 while en route to Indian Territory. The fringed buckskin leggings of 'Long Jack' and the designs on the baldrics of 'Inspector General' are consistent with surviving Seminole material in museums. Bands of neck beads are still worn by Florida Seminole women today.

Seminoles, some of whom were allowed to stay in the Everglades, has grown the present Seminole population of Florida. In the West the Seminoles refused to join the Creeks; they established their own capital at Wewoka and have a record of orderly assimilation to white rural culture, although their lands were allotted and melted away during the Oklahoma land grab. Today 8,000 Seminoles remain in Oklahoma, and over 2,000 in southern Florida. A few Seminoles and Seminole-Blacks established small colonies in Texas and Mexico.

Bibliography

Conn, Richard, *Native American Art in the Denver Art Museum*, Denver Art Museum, 1979.

Densmore, Frances, *Seminole Music*, Bulletin 161, Bureau of American Ethnology, Smithsonian Institution, Washington DC, 1956.

Fundaburk, Emma Lila, *Southeastern Indians Life Portraits*, Scarecrow, Reprint Corporation, Metuchen, New Jersey, 1969.

Hodge, William H., *The First Americans then and now*, Holt, Rinehart and Winston, 1981.

Howard, James H., *Choctaw Music and Dance*, University of Oklahoma Press, Norman, 1990.

Lewis, Thomas M.N. and Kneberg, Madelaine, *Tribes That Slumber*, The University of Tennessee Press, 1958.

McKenney, Thomas and Hall, James, *The Indian Tribes of North America* (3 vols.), John Grant, Edinburgh, 1934.

Medford, Claude, *Southeast Indian Buckskin Making*, American Indian Crafts and Culture Magazine vol. 5, no. 6, June 1971.

Mooney, James, *Myths of the Cherokee*, 19th Annual Report of the Bureau of American Ethnology, Smithsonian Institution, Washington DC, 1900.

Peithmann, Irvin M., *The Unconquered Seminole Indians*, Great Outdoors, St Petersburg, Florida, 1957.

Pierite, Joseph A., *Present Day Crafts of the Tunica and Biloxi Tribes of Louisiana*, American Indian Crafts and Culture Magazine vol. 8, no. 3, March 1974.

Sturtevant, William C., *Seminole Men's Clothing*, reprint from essays on the verbal and visual arts proceedings of the 1966 Annual Spring Meeting of the American Ethnological Society, University of Washington Press, 1967.

Swanton, John R., *Early History of the Creek Indians and their Neighbours*, Bureau of American Ethnology, Bull. 73, Smithsonian Institution, Washington D.C., 1922.

Swanton, John R., *Indian Tribes of the Lower Mississippi Valley and adjacent Coast of the Gulf of Mexico*, BAE, Bull. 43, Smithsonian Institution, Washington D.C., 1911.

Swanton, John R., The Indians of the Southeastern United States, BAE, Bull. 137, Smithsonian Institution, Washington DC, 1946.

Swanton, John R., *The Indian Tribes of North America*, BAE, Bull. 145, Smithsonian Institution, Washington DC, 1952.

Swanton, John R., *Social Organisation and Social Usages of the Indians of the Creek Confederacy*, 42nd Annual Report of the Bureau of American Ethnology, Smithsonian Institution, Washington DC, 1924–25.

Usner, Jnr., Daniel H., *Indians, Settlers & Slaves in a Frontier Exchange Economy: the Mississippi Valley before 1793*, The University of North Carolina Press, 1992.

Wood, Guy D., *Seminole Moccasins*, American Indian Crafts and Culture Magazine vol. 5, no. 3, March 1971.

THE PLATES

A: Adena and Hopewell

'Mound Builders' is a popular term for the prehistoric people who built earthen burial mounds, sometimes of impressive proportions, at first in the general area of the Ohio River valley but, subsequently, fanning out over much of eastern North America, beginning about 3,000 years ago. A people now termed 'Adena', so-called from the name of the estate near Chillicothe, Ohio, where a major site was discovered in 1901, built large cone-shaped mounds in which they buried their dead in bark-lined pits. Recovered grave goods include copper bracelets, shell beads, tobacco pipes, mica and stone ornaments. Serpent Mound in Ohio, so-called because of its snake effigy plan, is thought to have been the work of Adena-related people.

Hopewell culture, so-named from the Ohio farmer on whose land archaeologists found one of the richest of all burial mounds, appeared about 2,300 years ago (300 BC) and lasted for 800 years. Its influence extended throughout eastern North America via a vast network of trade in goods, stimulated by burial ceremonialism, including daggers, knives of obsidian, sheet copper, mica cut in the form of birds, serpents, human hands which were committed to the burial mounds. They were hunters and gatherers, but agriculture which perhaps appeared in the Adena period became important and links them tentatively with ancient Mexico.

Seminole chief, Billy Bowlegs, during the Third Seminole War (1855–58). He wears a silver headband with traded ostrich feathers and sashes of beadwork. He has a number of descendants among present-day Seminole people. From an early photograph or daguerreotype c. 1858, perhaps taken in New Orleans en route to Indian Territory with his band.

A1: Adena priest, c. 500–200 BC
Wearing a bear headdress, a snake ornament on his chest and holding an obsidian blade.

A2: Hopewell priest, c. AD 300–500
Wearing a copper antler headdress with river pearls and a feather cloak, based on archaeological remains.

A3: Hopewell woman, c. AD 300
Hairstyle based on recovered sculptures.

A4: Hopewell man, c. AD 300
Pipe and bear ornament on his chest.

A5: Hopewell platform pipes, c. 100 BC–AD 400

Platform pipes of steatite in the form of birds and animals.

B: Mississippian

About AD 700 new cultural stimulus from Mexico infiltrated north to the people of the fertile bottom lands of the Mississippi River and its tributaries, helping to develop a culture heavily involved in the planting and harvesting of Indian corn (maize). This culture, termed 'Mississippian', subsequently increased corn production so that it was able to support a city of 30,000 people at Cahokia, Illinois, where a huge man-made flat-topped pyramid of earth over 100 ft high was erected. Mississippian mounds were surmounted by temples, no longer just burial mounds. From Spiro (Oklahoma) in the west to Ocmulgee (Georgia) in the east, substantial quantities of pottery, pipes, engraved conch shells and figurines have been unearthed along with a great proliferation of grave goods associated with the 'Death Cult' complex at a number of sites. Native copper was fashioned into ornate headdresses, plaques, ear spools and celts and craftsmen engraved intricate designs on shells imported from the Gulf Coast depicting dancers in ceremonial attire. The culture survived up to the time of the first European exploration in the early 16th century and, although on the wane, a form survived to be seen by the French when encountering the Natchez, whom they destroyed in 1729.

B1: Chunkey player ready to throw his spear, c. 1200–AD 1500

B2: Chunkey player about to roll the disc – the 'chunkey'

Chunkey was a form of the widespread American Indian game of hoop and spear, played by the Mississippians and by the historic Choctaws and Creeks during the 18th century when witnessed by white traders. The disc was rolled ahead and players threw spears or poles at the moving target – the closer the spear landed to the disc at rest the higher the points the thrower scored. The game was played on specially prepared fields – called 'chunkey yards'. The players' kilts and belt-sashes are known from depictions on engraved shells recovered from archaeological sites.

B3: Birdman dancer, c. AD 1200–1500

Engraved conch shells excavated from the Mississippian sites have allowed us to reconstruct the ceremonial dress of dancers, which included roach-like hair, forelock decoration, sashes, belts and knee bands. Characteristic are the feathered wings attached to the arms and painted faces with particular emphasis on the eye probably representing the falcon, a bird with a formidable hunting and killing speed of attack – and thus perhaps connected with the 'Southern' or 'Death' cult.

B4: Mississippian priest, c. AD 1200–1500

The importance of death ritual and sacrifice, which goes back to Adena culture with decapitation with ceremonial clubs widespread, reinforces the link with ancient Mexico.

C: Mississippian and the 16th century
C1: Spiro warrior in armour, c. AD 1250.

Adapted from a sculpture from the Spiro mound in Oklahoma, the western outpost of Mississippian culture. He wears a helmet and armour (possibly copper) and holds a club made from a single piece of polished stone.

C2: Mississippian woman from Tennessee, c. AD 1250

Based on a figurine from a Tennessee grave site. Shows a woman with plaited hair, a headband and a short apron.

C3: Spiro man, c. AD 1200–1350

He wears an elaborate headdress, feather cloak, shell ear decoration depicting the 'Long-Nosed God', based on a sculpture recovered from the Mississippian site in Oklahoma, carved from brick-red bauxite of a seated man with hands on knees and a bowed head. The Spiro people may have been Caddoan ancestors.

C4: Timucua man, c. 1564

C5: Timucua woman, c. 1564

The Timucua figures are derived from the drawings of Jacques Le Moyne who accompanied the French Huguenot colonists to northern Florida in 1564, ousted by the Spanish shortly afterwards. Le Moyne escaped and later produced a number of watercolours depicting Timucuan people. John White, the English artist who accompanied English settlers to Roanoke Island in 1585, in present-day North Carolina, returning twice, made similar paintings of the local Algonkians (*Powhatans*). The works of both White and Le Moyne were published in 1590 and 1591 respectively by the Flemish engraver and publisher Theodore de Bry. However, two paintings of Timucuans are attributed to White, but Le Moyne inspired or copied. The tattooed Timucua man wears a headdress probably of raccoon fur and metal objects possibly Spanish gold or native traded copper. Shell or stone pendants hang from his belt. The woman, also tattooed, wears a Spanish moss skirt. Missionised by the Spanish and destroyed by the English, the Timucuans are extinct.

C6: Key Marco – wooden sculptures, c. AD 900–1400

A group of remarkable wooden sculptural remains have been salvaged from the mud-water environment of Marco Island, southern Florida. Possibly the work of the Calusa people or their ancestors whose linguist and cultural connections with other southeastern Indians or Caribbean Indians remains a matter of debate.

D: Southern Indians visit London, 1734

The commercial interests of England's southern colonies South Carolina and Georgia required the friendly relationship with the interior Indian peoples and consequently the British undertook formal treaties with the various tribes whom they considered separate nations. To cement these relationships three important official delegations of Southern Indians visited London in the 18th century. A group of Cherokee Indians led by Sir Alexander Cuming visited London in 1730; a group of Creeks led by James Oglethorpe (founder of Georgia) in 1734 and a party of Cherokee in 1762 led by Lieutenant (later Major) Henry Timberlake. The party of 1734 included a Lower Creek leader named Tomochichi, his wife, nephew and several others, seen here walking in a London park. At this time for some unknown reason he had been outlawed by his own people and had settled with his followers at a place called Yamacraw close to Savannah. Subsequently reconciled with his people, he helped to effect a treaty

Two Cherokee men painted by William Hodges RA in London in 1790–91, who accompanied William Augustus Bowles during an 'unofficial delegation' of Cherokee and Creek Indians to London to re-establish commercial and military activity between Great Britain and the southern tribes following the American Revolution. Bowles was a Tory American born on the Maryland frontier in 1763 who had lived and married among the Creeks. He was in the Bahamas after the American Revolution but subsequently returned to live with the Creeks. The two Cherokees may have been the mixed bloods Moses Price and Richard Justice. Moses was still living in 1799 at Coyotee Old Town at the mouth of the Little Tennessee River. Bowles died in a Havana prison in 1805. The Cherokees are wearing silver ear spools and gorgets, with trade blankets carried on their shoulders. (Courtesy of the Royal College of Surgeons, London, UK)

between the Lower Creeks and the Georgia colony. He died in October 1739 and was given a public funeral at Savannah.

The Creeks' attire in London is based on the painting by Verelst in 1734; Tomochichi's wife, D1, wears English dress. Tomochichi, D2, has a tattooed face and chest and wears a fur robe. Another male member of the party with the bear cub holds a 'calumet', a form of ceremonial pipe smoked to solemnise treaties of friendship.

E: 18th century
E1: Cherokee man, c. 1790

Our knowledge of the dress of Cherokee men before 1800 is limited but it was a combination of European and Indian materials. They adopted the frontiersman's open-fronted coat, either of cloth or buckskin with a shawl-like shoulder cape, and wore silver ear spools and gorgets. The Cherokee made fine finger-woven belts and sashes, replacing native fibres with yarn and wool. They also made woven beaded belts and wampum belts with glass beads of the white traders. Their moccasins were the type known throughout eastern North America, being the soft-soled variety of buckskin with a central front seam over the instep. The Cherokee and Choctaw used the cane blowgun with poisoned darts for hunting, which had a range of over 30 ft.

E2: Koasati-Creek man, c. 1790

The culture and dress of the large interior southeastern tribes had become a vigorous mixture of European and native elements, reflected in the use of cloth turbans, silver gorgets, ear and nose rings, military coats, cloth leggings – but retaining the indigenous front seam. Beaded belts sometimes used designs in bilaterally symmetrical 'ladder-like' forms. The Koasati were linguistically only distantly related to the true Muskogi Creeks – but came to be considered as part of the Upper Creeks – of Alabama and removed west of the Mississippi to Indian Territory (Oklahoma) and Louisiana during the early 19th century where descendants are still found. This figure is based partly on a sketch by John Trumbull when a group of Creeks visited New York in 1790.

E3: Tunica chief, c. 1735

Tribal life of the lower Mississippi area diminished following the conflict between the French and Natchez in 1729, with intertribal animosities exacerbated by colonial activity. Here a Tunica chief with war-paint carries three Natchez scalps on his staff. He is based upon a contemporary French sketch.

E4: Atakapa warrior, c. 1735

The Atakapa tribes were scattered in present-day southern Louisiana and adjacent coastal Texas. They had a reputation for cannibalism. Their eastern bands, and the Opelousas, were by 1754 firmly involved with French traders and diminished rapidly. By 1885 only a few people of Atakapa origin remained near Lake Charles and amongst the Creole population of Calcasieu Parish, Louisiana. The warrior shown is based upon the drawing of Alexandre de Batz indicating face paint, distinctive hair style, and trade cloth breechclout.

F: Second Seminole War 1835–42

The Seminoles (a name probably derived from the Spanish 'cimarron' meaning 'wild') were originally Creeks who moved to Florida during the 18th and early 19th centuries, at first from the Lower Creek towns of Georgia and later, following the Creek War with the Americans, 1812–14, from the Upper Creek towns of Alabama. Florida, then still Spanish territory until transferred to the US in 1819 (although the transfer was not completed until 1821) was considered a safe haven for the newcomers and runaway black slaves who formed separate, but politically integrated, Seminole towns. The Americans invaded Spanish Florida between 1816 and 1818, attacking Seminole and black towns in the first of three wars. The Second Seminole War 1835–42, was one of the most bitter and costly Indian campaigns ever undertaken as the Americans attempted to remove the Indians from the Florida peninsula to Indian Territory. After the capture of Osceola, Wild Cat or Coacoohee continued the guerilla warfare until his surrender in 1841. Between 1855 and 1858 the remaining Seminoles waged a last-ditch fight against removal under Billy Bowlegs and Aripeka or Sam Jones in the Florida swamps. Bowlegs was persuaded to move but Jones and his band remained in Florida.

F1: Seminole warrior, c. 1836

He wears a cloth turban with traded ostrich plumes, an open-fronted coat, bandanna and shirt of traded calico, gingham, cotton or flannel. His sash and garters are of finger-woven wool with interspaced beads and his bandolier of red trade cloth has typical Seminole curvilinear beadwork designs.

F2: Seminole warrior, c. 1836

His dress includes crescentic silver gorgets suspended around his neck, silver headband, buckskin coat with beadwork and ribbon edging, buckskin moccasins and leggings. His face paint consists of red war-paint representing blood, green which enabled better night sight, and yellow for death.

F3: Black Seminole guide, c. 1836

Black auxiliaries and scouts had fought with their Seminole hosts after escaping from Southern plantations, often adopting Indian dress, language and customs. He wears a red cloth bandolier.

F4: Seminole warrior, c. 1836
Stripped as for combat, he wears a truncated triangular cloth breechclout.

G: 19th century
G1: Creek chief, c. 1826
During the early 19th century leaders of the Southern tribes were regular visitors to Washington, negotiating treaties in the vain attempt to halt American settlement of their lands. Many were painted by the artist Charles Bird King (1785–1862) and his associate George Cooke. King was the official government painter of these Indian delegations. Despite the loss of many of the original works in a fire at the Smithsonian Institute, Washington DC in 1865, copies both by King himself and Henry Inman (for the plates used in the 3-volume epic *History of the Indian Tribes of North America* by McKenney and Hall) have survived. The Creek chief shown, partly based on the McKenney and Hall plates, shows him wearing a caped open-fronted coat, sash, belt, front seam leggings and moccasins. The triangular flap bandolier displays figurative beadwork, probably with spiritual representations. A number of Creek beaded objects have gold-plated beads.

G2: Eastern Cherokee booger dancers, c. 1900
Mask disguises were long ago widely used in ritual appeals for successful hunting and war, but only amongst the conservative Cherokee of North Carolina (a band who escaped removal and later occupied the Qualla or Eastern Cherokee Reservation) did mask making survive to the 19th and 20th centuries. Later Eastern Cherokee masks were called 'Booger Masks' and were worn during interludes in Cherokee social dances, their faces often displaying Euro-American characteristics thus regarded as clowns and the antithesis of Cherokee culture. Their function is therefore different to the masks of the Iroquois of the north, their long-distant relatives.

G3: Western Cherokee capitol building at Tahlequah, Indian Territory
Despite the tragedy of the relocation of the Cherokee, Creek, Choctaw, Chickasaw and Seminole to the new lands of Indian Territory (now Oklahoma), these so-called 'Five Civilized Tribes' made a remarkable adjustment to Euro-American culture,

A Miccosukee-Seminole woman of southern Florida c. 1980, working on quilted- or patchwork-decorated clothing. The descendants of the few Seminoles who remained in Florida after the three wars against the Americans are now divided into two groups: linguistically into those speaking Creek and those who speak Hitchiti (or Miccosukee); and recently, also politically, into two distinct 'tribes', the Miccosukee and Seminole.

the homes of mixed blood leaders and tribal capital buildings were modelled on southern styles. Some of these buildings, including the Cherokee capitol building, still survive as museums.

G4: Cherokee ball game player, c. 1890
Various forms of the ball game were played by eastern tribes from Hudson Bay to the Gulf of Mexico. It was played between two teams – sometimes representing villages, clans or moieties – on a field with goals set at a distance of several hundred yards. In the south the game was played with two ball sticks (rackets); the object was to drive the ball under the goal of the opposing team. The game was very rough and once used as a preparation for warfare; the Cherokee, Choctaw and Seminole still play the game today. The northern form of the game was adopted by Canadians under the name 'lacrosse'. Ceremonial scratching scars shown on the player's arm, performed by medicine men before the game, was considered beneficial to health and welfare.

G5: Stand Watie, Cherokee Confederate Brigadier General, 1865
The Western Cherokee of Indian Territory were divided into the old Ross and Ridge factions, the legacy of the removal which continued in the west with much bitterness with acts of murder and outlawry on both sides. At the outbreak of the Civil War in 1861 the Cherokee as slave owners were southern sympathisers. The old Ridge party headed by Stand Watie and their organisation 'Knights of the Gold Circle' declared for active service with the Confederacy whilst the Ross faction, supported by

their patriotic organisation the Kitoowah (Keetoo-wah) Society were for strict neutrality. Two Cherokee regiments were raised for Confederate service under Stand Watie and Colonel Drew, although the latter went over to the Union side after a dispute over service conditions. Stand Watie with 700 Cherokee and Creek men continued guerilla warfare through Arkansas, Kansas and Oklahoma and were among the last to lay down arms at the close of the war. The Keetoowah Society and derivative the 'Red Bird Smith' group are still organisations drawn from the conservative and predominantly full-blood Oklahoma Cherokees.

H: 20th century

H1: Oklahoma-Creek girl in ribbon dance dress, c. 1950

Creek women and girls wear this dress during the 'Busk' or Green Corn Dance and a part of the ceremony is descended from the women's scalp dance parades of the 18th century. Carrying knives indicates their willingness to prepare food. The Stomp Dance, derived from an old Creek and Cherokee ceremony, is the uniquely southeastern contribution to the 20th-century Pan-Indian dances of Oklahoma Indians. Primarily now a secular dance, the dress worn by girls consists of a blouse of a single colour with ribbon trim, a long, loose skirt with a light colour apron, both with ribbonwork. Long, wide ribbons are worn as pendants from the hair or blouse.

H2: Mississippi-Choctaw man, c. 1910

The ceremonial costume of the Choctaw is quite distinctive and is still worn for dances today. The flat hat or 'shapo' (*Chapeau*) is of Cajun influence, an open-fronted coat or today a collarless shirt is worn which usually has ribbonwork in contrasting colour on the front or arms. Belts and baldrics have beaded scroll or coiled snake and ball game designs which are of ancient origin. Silver armbands, silver gorgets and face paint were also items of male adornment no longer seen but remembered.

H3: Mississippi-Choctaw woman, c. 1980

The 'traditional' dress still worn by Choctaw girls in Mississippi on special occasions comprises a silver or beaded hair comb, a beaded necklace of net or open beadwork, a dress derived from the 19th-century styles with full sleeves, fitted top, long skirt of solid colour with ribbon appliqué work of contrasting colours. Over the dress is worn a long white apron with ruffles at bottom and sides. The Choctaw and other southeastern tribes excelled in basketry and the craft still persists.

H4: Florida-Seminole woman and child, c. 1915

The dress of the Florida Seminole of the late 19th and early 20th centuries developed into unique forms. Men wore long 'Big Coats' or knee-length tunics and women wore ankle-length dresses with a cape which later became a blouse, and many rows of neck beads. Dresses often had hand-sewn bands of contrasting coloured cloth around the lower part of the skirt. Between 1895 and 1910 Seminole women obtained hand-cranked sewing machines and replaced solid colour bands with bands of multi-coloured quilting or patchwork. Our model also wears coin silver brooches.

H5: Mississippi-Choctaw girl, c. 1910

Shows the origins of the modern Choctaw women's gala dress.

Three cloth bandoliers, probably Creek or Seminole c. 1830, decorated with beadwork. Although the interpretation of the designs are unknown, similar bags have human, animal, bird and other symbolic figures in abstract forms, which are also present here, despite being entirely constructed of trade materials. (From the permanent collection of the Montclair Art Museum, Montclair, New Jersey, USA)

INDEX

(References to illustrations are shown in **bold**. Plates are shown with page and caption locators in brackets.)